KU-660-867

ACROSS THE SPECTRUM

Spiritual Seekers Today

for
Ruth
a much valued fellow-worker in Christ
Ian Cowie

Ian Cowie

The Handsel Press

Published by
The Handsel Press Ltd
The Stables, Carberry, Musselburgh EH21 8PY

ISBN 1 871828 27 9

© 1993 The Handsel Press Ltd

All rights reserved. No part of this publication may be reproduced,
stored in retrieval system, or transmitted, in any form, or by any means,
electronic, mechanical, photocopying, recording or otherwise, without
the prior permission of the Handsel Press Ltd.

British Library Cataloguing -in- Publication Data
A Catalogue record for this book is available from the British
Library

Typeset in Times by Creative Link, Edinburgh
Printed by W.M.Bett Ltd, Tillicoultry

CONTENTS

Introduction: WHY THIS BOOK?

I can't usually be bothered with "Introductions", can you?

Yet this book needs one because a number of people to whom I have shown some parts of it... and there are too many to mention by name... have said something like this: "There's quite a lot that's interesting, Ian, but it is too personal. I can almost hear you speaking as I read it. A proper book is not like that. It should be more formal."

I did my best to be more formal, but it remains a personal book, arising out of experience, not out of books. The experience is of 30 odd years (some of them very odd!) as a Church of Scotland minister in industrial parishes, and 12 years with the Christian Fellowship of Healing in Edinburgh. As a parish minister and member of the Iona Community, I was always deeply involved in industrial, social and political issues and in relating the Gospel to them. It came as a bit of a surprise to find myself involved full-time with the Fellowship!

When I began with the Fellowship in 1977 there were a number of very charming, sincere people with spiritualist links who wanted me to lead the Fellowship on those lines. Then I was joined by some of my friends from the charismatic side. Then along came the New Age folk, mostly young and very sensitive, such sincere and lovable people! Their life-style often put me to shame. Then, not least, came my friends who had been in counselling and in the various semi-psychological aspects of pastoral care.

They were all people I respected, and admired. But they were incompatible with each other! Each wanted me to take his/her own line, and each was hurt when I did not. There was therefore real inner pain as I tried to work out what was what. This book is the fruit. I am still working on the problem, still aware that I leave many questions un-answered, but if I do not share it with you now, I never will! Perhaps it will prompt somebody else to carry on the exploration where I now leave off.

WHY BOTHER?

Because my experience shows me that there are large numbers of people who are seeking a spirituality of some sort with an open mind. The church as they know it seems to have nothing to interest them. They are put off by Charismatic emotionalism, and they see the more extreme New Agers as cranks. Yet I have found spiritual treasure within the ordinary church, within the Charismatic movement and in circles which many would label "New Age". I only wish that people would get together, drop the labels which they have stuck on each other, and share their insights *lovingly and without fear*.

Ian Cowie (Rev. J.L.Cowie)
Crosswise Cottage
16 Curate Wynd,
Kinross KY13 7DX

January 1993

Part I: THE ISSUES

1 THE NEW AGE

WHAT PEOPLE ARE SAYING

What is all this about a new age? Is it just the latest fad among the cranks? Or is there something truly NEW about our age? A number of very different people seem to think so. Here are some examples:

GEORGE MACLEOD

One of the great "prophetic" figures in our day has been George MacLeod, founder of the Iona Community. In 1942 he began his book *We Shall Rebuild* by affirming that we have come to the end of an age, and he would often say that "Christendom is at an end". The re-building of the ruined Abbey in Iona was from its inception a testimony to a new age in which we are called to "find new ways to touch the hearts of men". And long before we were aware of the "Charismatic Movement", he was speaking about our having moved into the "Age of the Spirit".

Those who read Ronald Ferguson's remarkable biography of him will see how long ago it was that George was proclaiming that the vital issue in the new age would be a new attitude to "matter" and that it was vital for us to find a new, Christ-centered attitude to it. He often expressed this in ways which seemed "way out" to sensible theologians, yet in this as in many things he was decades ahead of his time.

DIETRICH BONHOEFFER

A few years after George MacLeod had set his hand to the plough in Iona, Dietrich Bonhoeffer, imprisoned by the Nazis, was writing of how Western man had "come of age", and that this called for a radically new understanding of what it meant to be a Christian.

W.S.ROBERTSON

After the war, one of the industrialists who helped to put Scotland's industry back on its feet was W.S.Robertson. He wrote a small book which I have to quote from memory, for I cannot trace a copy or remember its title. He maintained that humanity had come to a "critical point". To explain that term we turn to water. H_2O may come as ice, but there is a "critical point" as one raises the temperature, and it becomes a liquid. There is another "critical point" if we heat it further at which it becomes water vapour. It has radically changed its form while remaining the same thing. This is what the term "critical point" refers to.

He asserted that humanity had reached such a "critical point". Hitherto our science and knowledge were aimed at helping us to survive in, and to adapt to our environment, which seemed to have unlimited resources. Religion had helped our ancestors to come to terms with the inexplicable. But now we know that we are in control of our environment and could destroy it. Our religion must be concerned about how we can save the earth from being destroyed by human greed. There is a new agenda for us all.

MAGNUS PYKE

A few years later Magnus Pyke in his book *Nothing like Science* made the point that automation and artificial intelligence are far more than just a new set of gadgets. He maintained that scientific advances will completely alter our understanding of what life is about... another pointer to a "new age".

HAROLD LOUKES

From a very different point of view we have a Quaker, Harold Loukes. In his book *The Castle and the Field**, he made the point that so far the churches have been sniping at each other and at the world from CASTLE positions. Each church had built up defensive armour of texts and theologies, and each was sure of having a monopoly of God. Yet this ecclesiastical Maginot Line has been left behind. In our day the spiritual warfare is out in the FIELD where everything is on the move. The old "prepared positions" and ready-made answers are now irrelevant, he maintained. We have moved into an age in which many of what we once considered basic defences are now ancient monuments... a new age again!

*Swarthmore Lectures 1959

GORDON STRACHAN

Those who go in for astrology also speak of a new age, the age of Aquarius, the one who pours water, and those who look at it from a Christian point of view see this as a symbol of the Holy Spirit, as explained in *Christ and the Cosmos* by Gordon Strachan.

4

IN THE MELTING POT

One could go on quoting people rom very different backgrounds who have perceived that we ARE moving into a new age in which the very fundamentals have to be re-thought. Perhaps we should simply try to come to terms with it. Those of us who believe in God should believe that it is HE who makes all things new. It is Jesus who calls us to re-think radically. (What a pity that the Greek for "re-think" is translated as "repent"! He does not ask us to become morbidly obsessed with our sins, but to re-think our positions in the light of the Good News that "JESUS IS LORD!")

Just as, about 500 years ago, the movement which we call THE RENAISSANCE hit Europe, and had all sorts of results, some good, some bad, so it seems that we live in an age when once more everything is going into the melting pot. What we know as the scientific outlook was born in the Renaissance and what we call the NEW AGE movement is indeed a re-thinking of this outlook in its turn. The crucial issue as outlined by George MacLeod so many decades ago, is whether Christians can rise to proclaim Christ in such a way as to save the New Age movement from going wrong.

Of course, predictably, there are those who react to all the above assertions by building up their "castles" even more strongly. There are those who escape into taking up the position which says that since Jesus is going to come back at any moment, there is no point in re-thinking our attitude to the earth, since, according to them, it will soon be destroyed anyway. This is a "cop-out" which is very popular in America, especially among those with "good reason" not to want to re-think their very prosperous situation.*

* "He shall come again to judge the living and the dead" is part of the basic belief of the church. But remember that the word JUDGE in the Bible means to administer justice, i.e. to rule. The conclusion of such a belief, Jesus tells us, is that we should be conscientiously getting on with the work he gave us to do, and our marching orders in Genesis 1:26 remain: we have to rule the earth, making it fruitful, seeing that the strong do not exploit the weak, and that harmony is maintained. Every species that becomes extinct is a black mark against us! The trouble with people who have become unbalanced in their anticipation of his Coming, is that they usually draw the wrong conclusion, and write off their responsibility to the earth.

Many of us, however, who are firmly grounded in the faith handed down from the prophets and apostles, know the need to go back to fundamentals; from there, we should re-think everything, if we are to move into this new age without finally destroying the planet, which, according to Genesis 1:26, God has told us to take care of for Him.

Few, however, would dream of trying to work out this new line within the local church as we know it, for it seems to most people either dull and formal, or else narrow and bigoted. Neither variety seems to have the tang of Jesus of Nazareth. Neither seems aflame with that costly love which is the "salt of the earth", the only thing which can stop life on earth from going rotten. (Salt in Jesus' day was mainly a preservative, not a matter of taste.)

SEEKERS

Meanwhile outwith the church there are deep changes going on in the general consciousness of people. More and more people have come to have a deep concern for the earth and its creatures, and a profound feeling that we have gone badly wrong in our dealings with them.

On the other hand we find many who have grown up with a deep feeling that there are beings in the universe other than ourselves. Whether they see these beings in terms of science fiction or whether they see them in terms of more ancient mythology, it matters little. Such people also have a profound feeling that we have gone badly wrong.

These seekers are not, however, usually drawn to the conventional churches. Yet they do seek others who share their concern, and they seek wisdom which will help them to develop these deep feelings. We have to remember, too, that many of these earnest seekers have only misleading fragments of knowledge about the Christian faith and are generations removed from the church. The approach to them must be different from the approach to those who have grown up with Christian teaching, and rejected it. The new generation has an open-ness to anything which makes sense, without any preconceived idea that Christianity is a "good thing".

One cannot help but feel that, to use the words of Jesus, "the harvest is ready for reaping". There is throughout western society today a widespread and deep sense of sin, even though most people would reject the use of this word... perhaps because in the past it has been so sex-related. However this sense that we have gone badly wrong is very much in line with what the Bible means by sin. Yet conventional churches fail to see this as an opening for the Gospel. They fail to see too that the Bible is full of an awareness of non-human intelligent

6

beings, and aware that there is a right and a wrong attitude to them.
Western, protestant pictures of "angels" and "cherubs" and the like do
little to help! Once again we fail to see the opening offered by sensitive
people rebelling against a dead materialism, seeking ways to express a
truth which they sense deep within.

It seems that a wide hole has been blown in the anti-Christian
materialistic world-view, and all sorts of people are exploring through
it into new areas. Rather than deploring this, Christians should be
seeing that they have much to learn, much to re-think, and good news
to proclaim to those who seek. Only so will they be ready to enter
gloriously into whatever is ahead.

It is all very well to say, as one anti-New Age booklet says, that
such people are seeking for an easy spirituality, but that is to miss the
point. Very often such seekers find themselves having to change their
life-style more than most Charismatics would. Many give up "good
jobs", travel far and read widely in their search for a spirituality. The
tragedy is that the Christian Church is often the last place they think of
looking. To blame the seekers is to miss the point yet again.

Therefore we must now look at the New Agers and the
Charismatics.

NEW AGERS

It is not surprising if some people begin to explore in the so-
called "New Age" direction. Those who do become "New Agers"
develop a real concern for the ecological crisis, with its demand for
simpler living. They also become aware that people of other cultures
have much to teach Europeans and Americans, even if the latter do
claim to be Christian. Many who verge towards the New Age end keep
their basic Christian faith intact, in fact they would maintain that their
awareness of who Christ is has been deepened. Others, with no
religious background, are finding that the New Age outlook is their first
step on the way to a spiritual understanding, drawn, we would say, by
the Holy Spirit.

ALTERNATIVE MEDICINE

One very prominent feature of the New Agers is their concern
for holistic medicine and natural therapies. We shall be looking at this
in more detail later, but let us just note that they see the normal medical
profession as being "reductionist"; it reduces the human being to an

assembly of parts, but ignores the whole person.

If we read New Age literature we find a bewildering variety of therapies from all over the world pouring out like a steady stream. There are always new ideas, new people with some wonderful technique or medicine. One thinks of acupuncture, reflexology, massage, colour therapy, herbal remedies, diagnosis by pendulum, energy fields and so on *ad infinitum*.

In most books popular with Charismatic Christians all these are listed as Satanic seductions, while offering little critique of modern medicine. We shall therefore have to look at many of these things item by item, trying to see both sides, steering between naivety and bigotry.

THE SELF

Another feature of the New Agers is that they are very much "into" techniques and systems to aid help develop self-knowledge, self-awareness, self-acceptance, self-expression and so on. They use astrology and many semi-psychological techniques to help them come to terms with themselves. In books such as *Psychology as Religion* (Paul C. Vitz) a warning is sounded from the evangelical side that these techniques may lead us to avoid the real need for us to repent of our sins (we have mentioned the real meaning of 'repent' already!) and to be remade by the Holy Spirit; it is putting the cart before the horse to say: "I'll get myself right first, then I'll start thinking about God". However, in fairness one would have to comment that some who shout loudest about being Christian could do with a little self-knowledge!

This pre-occupation with self can go wrong like anything else, especially if SELF remains central to living, so let us not write off the criticism too readily, but neither let us ignore some very basic modern forms of wisdom.

DIABOLIC?

One reads, however, in various Christian books and magazines of alarming developments in the New Age movement:

* **The replacement of the Gospel by a watered-down oriental-psychological religion based on a world-figure who is to replace Jesus.**

* **The reinstatement of the old pre-Christian gods to replace the God and Father of our Lord Jesus Christ.**

* **Involvement with deep occult practices, and "Luciferic initiation", Lucifer being another name for the Devil.** (Basileia Schlink's booklet *New Age* is widely circulated and sums up this point of view.)

There are, no doubt, some people who are involved in such extremes, many of them unbalanced... if they were not when they started, they soon become so. We have had to deal with some such, and know to our cost how profoundly confused people can become when they get involved with some of the deeper aspects of New Age ideas.

Yet the young people who, for instance come to work in the Abbey in Iona, moved by what they have gathered about the New Age, are not like that at all. They are open to the Gospel if it is proclaimed in a way which they can understand. Sickened by the life they have seen around them, they have set out on a spiritual search, not knowing where it will lead them, like Abraham of old. The last thing they need is somebody to tell them that they are satanic!

CHARISMATICS

However, while some people, of all ages and backgrounds, find themselves moving in the New Age direction, others have reacted into the Charismatic movement, with its warm, emotional worship, and with its demand for a more costly obedience. Here again we find many who are main-line members of the churches, but who have realized that we have indeed entered into the Age of the Spirit. Let us now look at some of the "Charismatic" features.

THE GIFTS OF THE SPIRIT

Healing and other spiritual Gifts make it plain that "God is for real". It is a wonderful step forward when a congregation discovers that the Gifts of the Spirit are REAL, and given to ordinary people, enabling them to find a ministry. Such a congregation is no longer a collection of passive listeners to Mr So-and-so's sermons, but actively shares in the work of the Spirit.

However just as the New Agers can get lost in a welter of new ideas, so the Charismatics can become tied in knots over the niceties of the Gifts of the Spirit, losing contact with reality... and God is always in reality, not in our theories! Only too often spiritual pride creeps in and it all becomes divisive. However here are two of the positive features.

FELLOWSHIP AND HEALING

Jesus said that love for one another should be the true mark of his Church, but you might not think that to look at a normal congregation! However when a Charismatic congregation meets there is a lot of hugging and kissing, a real warmth of emotion, and singing which appeals to people who have grown up with "pop" music. People minister to each other, and get very involved with one anothers' problems, unlike the average congregation in which sharing emotion is taboo!

Charismatics are of course very strong in their belief in the healing power of the Holy Spirit at work through the Christian fellowship. Most of them regard alternative medicine as evil, but accept normal medicine uncritically. In fact one finds many nurses and doctors in Charismatic fellowships and churches.

THE DEVIL

One feature is that Charismatics take the devil and demons seriously, although, strangely, they seem less concerned with angels! However they have recovered a whole area of psychic reality of which most ministers know nothing. But once more we find extremists, for whom this important aspect of the Christian life, "spiritual warfare", has become an obsession.

There is a real tendency for such groups to become very inward-looking, tending to see everything but their own little set-up as "of the devil". Some such fellowships seem to spend most of their time exorcising each other, and talking about satanic attacks. They become as devil-centered as the extreme New Age folk without realising it!

It is easy to dismiss the whole Charismatic, renewal movement on account of these extremists, just as others dismiss the whole New Age movement because of its extremists. We must try to work out for ourselves what is good and bad in both, and find our own way forward in this exciting age.

TODAY'S TENSIONS

To clarify the issue, let us look at two groups of people and at what the Americans call "the interface" between the two. They are both known to me, and perhaps you too could think of people whom you know like this.

NEW AGE COMMUNITY

The first group is a small community, each of whom once had a well-paid job. They gave up their jobs in order to live together in a simple "Sermon on the Mount" style. They are a very caring and sharing "family", making beautiful and useful things, trying to help the people in the nearby village learn crafts and skills which will enable them to resist the drift to the city. They do not insist on those who wish to join them being "Christian", but accept all comers "just as they are", so long as they fit in.

THE CHARISMATIC CONGREGATION

It is a very large congregation, with a high proportion of young people. They believe that the "Gifts of the Spirit" (tongues, prophecy, healing and so on, as in 1 Corinthians 12) are for the church today. They fill the church several nights a week with praise and loving fellowship. Those who have become fully committed to the fellowship have a strong discipline, including tithing their incomes. In their enthusiasm for their new Way, they are very keen that everybody who comes should have the same experience and the same doctrinal beliefs, and while they accept anybody, they do exert much more pressure on those who come in from the outside than the New Age people do, and they make it clear that if one does not conform, then one is "lost."

Both these groups are very alive, and it would appear that both are the work of the Holy Spirit. Yet they look upon each other with deep suspicion! The Charismatics see the New Age folk as satanic because they are "into" astrology, use a pendulum for diagnosis, and experiment with oriental forms of meditation.

The New Age folk would (I guess) look aghast at the long line of cars outside the church each night, and at the lack of awareness of the ecological crisis among the Charismatics. They would be horrified at the evidence in Charismatic homes that the occupants are keeping up with the Joneses very effectively and by no means in an eco-friendly way.

Most of the people in both groups grew up in homes with at least a church background, but have rejected it as having nothing to say to them, nothing that seems relevant to the world as they see it. There are also in each group those who come in from outside, from a totally non-religious background and have found the need to discover the spiritual dimension.

11

What the people in the above groups have in common is: the need for direct spiritual experience which the normal church does not offer, and a togetherness which one does not find in a regular Sunday morning service.

Examining what Charismatics and New Age folk have in common and what they condemn in each other will take us into some very interesting areas, and will need some careful thought. So let us get down to work!

2 OURSELVES & OUR ENVIRONMENT

GETTING OUR AIM STRAIGHT

Having friends who have moved in the New Age direction and friends who have moved in the Charismatic direction, all of them deeply sincere, I offer this book in the hope that it will help us all to crystallize what is true, and to avoid meaningless arguments.

We shall try to work out basic principles to help us to sort out what is liable to go wrong in both movements and to evaluate what is good in both. We shall look for sign-posts pointing to worthwhile areas to explore, and warnings about the dangers to be encountered.

In some cases we will be able to see clearly what is right and what is wrong. In some cases I leave the questions open, for it seems to me that more work needs to be done.

On some matters we are not ready to be dogmatic - although some people would not agree with me in that, and would think that I am being dangerously "free-thinking". On the other hand I hope to show that a naive acceptance of any new thing is playing with fire - although some people would think I was being too conservative. If I draw fire equally from both sides, perhaps I may be somewhere near the truth!

Perhaps those who read this with a conventional church background but who feel the need to venture out of the old ecclesiastical "castles" (using Harold Loukes' illustration mentioned above) will find the courage to tackle warfare in the open country, even if their castle-bound friends express disapproval. (While God is our castle, as many of the psalms say, that is not to say that he is confined to the little shelters we build for him!)

Many today have been brought up with no Christian background, yet are beginning to explore the possibilities of a non-materialistic universe in this new age. I hope they will find some sign-posts which will help them find a reality in the Faith which perhaps they cannot find in the ordinary church. Perhaps they will find that there is more to the Gospel than they thought!

As an example of the sort of person I have in mind, I think of a young friend, a secondary school girl, who was reading with great interest a book on "out of the body experiences", complete with a do-it-yourself kit of instructions on how to allow your spirit to leave your body behind and to travel to different places. She was blissfully unaware of the psychic jungle into which she was heading, and mere ministerial disapproval would avail little. She would have to be given guide-lines such as few ministers are equipped to give. I hope that the thinking in this book* will save some people, such as her, from the sort of psychic disaster I have had to cope with in so many young people who have explored without a proper chart and compass, so to speak.

* I found that I was helped to understand much of this by Martin Israel, a South African Jew, lecturer at the London College of Surgeons, an Anglican priest, who is both a psychic and a mystic. *Summons to Life* and *The Spirit of Counsel* are two of his books which may help. And, since writing this book, I have read *The Quest for Wholeness* in which he makes many of the points which I make.

"WORDS, WORDS, WORDS!"

When sincere people with different points of view begin to discuss, one has to be careful not to be divided by "words". Deciding on a common vocabulary is a good starting point, and will prove quite a challenge to begin with! Only then can we agree on what the other person means, and then decide what is right and what is wrong.

To illustrate the confusion which can happen with words, my late father-in-law told me that when travelling in the also-late British Empire he had seen a crate with the legend:

TOP IS MARKED BOTTOM
TO AVOID CONFUSION

No doubt it did avoid confusion for somebody, but it leaves us with more than a hint of just that! Words have a nasty habit of doing this sort of thing, and people who are quite sure that they are speaking plainly find themselves misunderstood.

This is very much the case in the areas we are going to explore. For instance let us take the two words *Psychic, Spiritual*, and their "relations". You can find that not only do different people mean different things by a word such as "spiritual", but that a person can use "spiritual" with different meanings in one discussion without realising it.

To illustrate this further: one can find people enrolling for courses in "spiritual development" when it is really psychic development. On the other hand one can find Charismatic groups who do not realize how badly they have slipped from the spiritual level down to the psychic, even as they denounce spiritualists.

To avoid confusion, then, let us begin by getting some agreement about what we mean by certain terms. Many readers may think they have a better system, and I would not say that I am right and they are wrong, I only ask that in this book we make the best of what I suggest.

Humanity is like a valve: open to God above, and to the earth below. It was *through* humanity that God intended to develop the earth. Genesis 1-2 sees quite clearly that "THE MAN" (Hebrew: *A-DAM*) is in charge of the earth and of all that is in it. *ADAM* is right with God if he looks after the earth and its creatures properly, and if he is right with God he will do so .

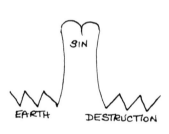

But as we know only too well, it has not worked out like that. Human beings are *self-centred* so that both God and the earth suffer, and we make each other suffer too. We are also liable to draw into ourselves the destructive forces at every level. The technical name for this self-centredness is "SIN", a word much misused.

At the highest level we human beings are *SPIRIT*, able to relate to God and to others, to make choices, to establish what we think is worthwhile (worship = worth-ship). Spirit is concerned with KNOWING (not knowing about, but person-to-person knowing). Spirit needs to find meaning in life and to *give* meaning to life. It has WILL-POWER.

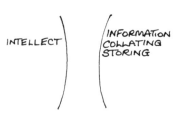

The next level is *INTELLECT*. We have an on-board computer which can handle facts. It can store them, re-call them, arrange them in different patterns and work out our problems. Once SPIRIT has set the aim, then INTELLECT works out how to get there. We generally reckon that it is the brain which does this.

Now we come down to the *PSYCHE*, to use the Greek word. It is the warm, emotional, feeling aspect of us, and a lot of what we think of as "personality" centres around this. When it goes wrong, it is this aspect of us that is dealt with by PSYCHotherapists and by PSYCHiatrists. All the arts depend on our psychic element, as it pushes upwards, so to speak, through intellect to spirit, and much of our emotional life comes from the interaction between the psychic and the animal nature, the physical.

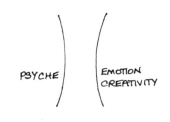

That brings us to the physical element, the *BODY*, made (in the dramatic words of Genesis) "from the dust of the earth". We all know, however, that at this level we share a lot with the animals. The body's functions are to *work creatively* in response to the SPIRIT, to *interact creatively* with others, and to *procreate* the species.

When the Gospel opens a person up to the love of God, then the Holy Spirit can flow in, activating us at every level:

16

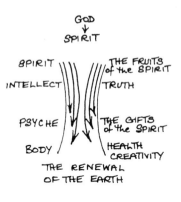

GOD
↓
SPIRIT

SPIRIT — THE FRUITS of the SPIRIT

INTELLECT — TRUTH

PSYCHE — THE GIFTS of the SPIRIT

BODY — HEALTH CREATIVITY

THE RENEWAL OF THE EARTH

* At the *spiritual* level we share the awareness which Jesus had at his Baptism: "This is my beloved son (daughter)" (Mark 1:11). We KNOW God as Father, and other people as our family. Hence "The Fruit of the Spirit" (Galatians 5:22-23).

* At the *intellectual* level the Spirit leads us into all truth (John 16:13).

* At the *psychic* level the Spirit gives "The Gifts of the Spirit" (1 Corinthians 12:5-11).

* At the *physical*, or bodily level we have true health.

You will notice that there are no horizontal lines between the various aspects, for they are not separable. For instance if I eat too much, I will find it hard to be as considerate and loving as I would want to be! On the other hand if my spirit is full of resentment and tension, my digestion may go on strike. We only make distinctions because we have problems! It is the same as with football...if my team is winning I am just aware of the game. However, if they lose I start thinking analytically about "team-work", "ball control", and "management". So in life: the object is to live as a totally integrated person, and it is the unity of the above elements which makes up a healthy life. We start analyzing only because we have become aware that things have gone wrong and that we are unhealthy.

You will notice that I do not mention *SOUL* in the above. I have read books which give varying versions of the difference between soul and spirit, but I do not find that any of them stand up to what we find in the Greek text of the New Testament. Personally I understand SOUL as referring to the total ME, from the cradle to the grave, that which "the resurrection body" will express. All the aspects in our diagram function in the time-space sequence, whereas "soul" is beyond time and space. But that is just my understanding, and it does not come into this book!

MIND is another word which I have omitted, because it is used in so many different ways.

IS THIS THE BIBLICAL VIEW?

This is what some folk will ask, and again I have to say that while I think it is, I am aware that almost every theologian has his own version of what the Bible means by the different words. One gets tied up with Hebrew and Greek. After all the Hebrews did not have abstract words, and they understood the parts of our bodies differently from us. For instance when the Psalmist writes about God inspecting his kidneys during the night, he means "reads my inmost mind." On the other hand when they refer to "heart" they mean intelligent thought, while "throat" means emotions. A literal Biblical view has complications!

THE ENVIRONMENT

Now let us come back to our "model" and look at it from another angle: at the environment rather than the interior make-up of human life. At each level of our being we have an environment to which we are relating all the time:

* At the *spiritual* level there are spiritual forces, sometimes called angels, and, as we shall see later, not always good. The other levels of our being often "shout louder" than the spiritual side so that we are not always aware of the spiritual forces around us. But nevertheless whether we know it or not, we are continually reacting to good and evil pressures in our spiritual environment. Christians call the latter "temptation".

* At the *intellectual* level we all do our thinking with ideas which circulate within our society. We are constantly bombarded with ideas, theories, words, information and so on. Once more they are not all good, and we have to try to sort out what is really true.

* At the *psychic* level we are continually aware of pressure, good or bad from other psyches. They create an "atmosphere", we say, and it affects us, either for good or for bad, often without our realising it. I would also put at this level many forces which people call "spirits", which is confusing, but we will look at that later. Our psychic awareness is often far greater than we think, and we might be surprised at how much we are influenced psychically by what is around us and by psychic experiences in the family's past.

One of the basic laws when dealing with things psychic is: **Like attracts like...** i.e.whatever is dominant in the hidden depths of your psyche, tends to attract similar influences in the psychic environment. This explains some surprising results when people experiment with meditation.

   *   At the *bodily* level we have the world, with everything from the vastness of space to the minute virus: here too there are destructive and constructive forces, and many which are constructive if rightly used, but destructive if wrongly used.

WHAT ABOUT GOD?

Shouldn't "God" be mentioned at the spiritual level? The answer is a very definite NO. Surprised? The reason is that God meets us at every level of our being, and there is always the danger of religious people trying to be more spiritual than God, as if the lower levels were really a rather unfortunate mistake. A lot of off-putting religion is suffering from this distortion. It results in "people being so heavenly minded that they are no earthly use". (Who said that first?)

You can read in many books which claim to be spiritual, teaching which suggests that what is spiritual is good, and that what is material is bad. In fact a lot of oriental religion is based on the assumption that the object of religion is to free the spirit from matter. One can even find subtle versions of this creeping into books which claim to be Christian, even though this is not really the understanding of the world which comes to us through the Gospel, which is about the *Word* of God *made flesh*. The human body therefore is not to be written off as a disposable, unworthy object. Rather it is to be hallowed as the Temple of the Holy Spirit, and it has a mysterious final destination "the resurrection of the body and the life everlasting", as the Creed puts it. ("Resurrection" does not mean the same as "resuscitation", whatever else it may mean).

If we avoid implying that the physical is in some way evil, we must avoid equally the mistake of thinking that what is spiritual is automatically good. The most dangerous sins are the spiritual ones. There is profound insight behind the simple story in Genesis 2, and nowhere more so than when it puts in the mouth of the tempter, "You shall be as gods". This is SPIRITUAL PRIDE, the fundamental human sin.* Typically, this pride leads to a subtle distortion of the truth about human destiny, and it is deadly.

It distorts the basic truth that humanity is indeed meant to be "in the image of God", but in the image of a God who is LOVE. We are indeed beings far more wonderful than we dream. But love, as St Paul writes in 1 Corinthians 13, "is never puffed up". Our true greatness lies in the greatness of our love, and things go wrong when this is distorted into the human desire to be boss of one's own life, and not to admit to being a creature. There are many ways of "playing at God": most of them seem to be right to the player!

It is at *this* spiritual level that everything else goes wrong, and all other wrongs and sins stem from this. So we see that good and evil, like God, meet us at every level of our being.

*In many books one may read that Christians believe that sex is the original sin, but this is quite wrong, even if some mediaeval monks did think so! Many people have swallowed a bad misrepresentation of Christian teaching here.

THE HUMAN EFFECT

Of course it is not only the environment which affects us at a deep level... we have our effect on the environment. In fact about 600 years ago, the author of *The Cloud of Unknowing* wrote:

> Let go! Give yourself entirely over to God's pleasure... the whole of mankind, in a most mysterious and wonderful way, will be helped by your action.

This is a staggering thought, and it counterbalances a tendency to be too inward-looking in our religion. We are meant to be radiating the love of God to our environment at every level, and if we are not doing so, then we are depriving not only the people around us, but the whole creation!

This means that whether we know it or not, we are having a far greater effect then we realize, for good or for evil, by what we do or by what we fail to do. We have to be responsible about this, then, so here is another basic guide-line to take into account:

The deeper one goes into the psychic and spiritual spheres the greater the effect on others at a level below consciousness.

To illustrate this, imagine a sermon preached by a minister who is full of the Holy Spirit, in a congregation which is prayerful, then imagine the same sermon read by an actor to an audience. In the first case there will be lives changed and people healed, in the second case people may find it interesting or even inspiring, but that is all. The words we actually hear are only the tip of the iceberg in the first case, the truly effective element is hidden.

Or again, take an example from every-day life: we have most of us known one or two people who are truly Christ-filled, and have a good effect on people around them without ever speaking about "religion". They are having an effect on people at the psychic and spiritual levels without any "religious" words being spoken. People say, "There's something about him, I don't know what it is, but I feel different when he's around". Of course eventually such people will be asked to "give a reason for the faith that is within them", but the verbal witness follows from the deep effect at the subconscious level. Those who *begin* by talking religion at the conscious level often have a negative effect.

On the negative side it also works. If groups of people are opening doors into the psychic areas through occult practices, through certain types of rock music or through drugs, they will be poisoning the whole atmosphere of society. This may well explain some of the unpleasant things we see today. Since in most places these days there are groups doing these things, it underlines the importance of parish worship, for this affects not only the people who attend, but the whole life of the parish, and counteracts the evil effect of other practices.

We have to be clear, however, that we cannot divide people up into goodies and baddies. Even the best Christian can slip up to temptation and begin to radiate negativity. The stronger that person has been as a "transmitter" of goodness, the more dangerous he or she is when off-beam. For instance if one goes to a service and instead of coming away uplifted, one comes away drained, it may well be because the minister or some "pillar of the kirk" has slipped, and the whole congregation and community suffer a negative effect. On the other hand, of course, it may be that it is oneself who has slipped! (For a deeper understanding, see the work of Jung, or read Laurens van der Post's biography of Jung.)

Our picture of ourselves, then, is that of a living organism, open to God and working upon the earth, inter-relating all the time with our environment at many levels.

At every level there is conflict and danger, and it is in and through this struggle that we grow into the likeness of God, and that is what life is about... From a Christian point of view, God's love for humanity, and indeed for the world, has involved getting personally involved in the danger and in the pain of the struggle, coming to terms with it at its worst on the Cross.

21

3 PUTTING OUR MODEL TO WORK

PSYCHICS, MYSTICS & SPIRITUALISTS

To clear up some confusion, first let us look at the word *PSYCHIC*. We say that a person is "psychic" if he/she seems to have an ability to communicate with other psyches without using the normal senses. Of course we all have psyches, so we are all psychic in one sense, but popular usage has narrowed the meaning. It would seem that psychics have a thinner psychic "skin" than most, and so can sense things which others cannot. It seems to run in families, and is neither good nor bad in itself. It does make people very susceptible to outside influences, and is often far from being a blessing. People who are psychic need special care, and it does not help if, as in some books, it is suggested that they are "possessed".

The next step is to look at the difference between the words *PSYCHIC* and *MYSTIC*. With the aid of our model we can distinguish between MYSTICAL EXPERIENCES, at the spiritual level, in which the person communes with God directly, and PSYCHIC EXPERIENCES which may involve communication with beings of a much lower order, earth-forces, E.S.P., telepathy, "spirits of the departed" and so on. (The term "spiritualist" is misleading.)

We can also see why, as we have already noted, we must also beware of those who claim to offer "spiritual development" or to teach "spiritual healing" when they actually are developing psychic sensitivity, often to a pitch which the person cannot handle spiritually.

Here is a basic guideline: **A person truly focused upon God in faith and in love, will be given such psychic elements as are needed. People who deliberately develop psychic sensitivity on its own are in real danger.**

Finally we look at the word *SPIRITUALIST*. (We shall look at spiritualism in more detail later.) In the meantime we have to be clear that being psychic does not mean that one is a SPIRITUALIST. For clarity, note that spiritualists are people who believe that it is right to contact the dead by means of a medium or "sensitive" and who take part in such activities. Some of these claim to be Christian, some very definitely reject Christianity.

On the other hand, most of those who attend seances etc. are not "psychic" themselves, but depend on the medium who has developed his or her psychic side. **Some folk are psychic but not spiritualist,**

while others are spiritualist but not psychic.

There is a very definite, practical pastoral side to this, for many families experience some sort of psychic phenomena at the time of a death in the family. One often finds them puzzled and frightened, but afraid to mention it to their minister or priest, lest they be thought spiritualist. In this way a very real pastoral opportunity is missed, for if it is linked in with sound spiritual teaching, then the psychic experience can enrich them and lead them into a spiritual experience. However if the minister fights shy, or even rebukes them, as I have known to happen, then they are left frightened and open to those who will interpret things differently. Perhaps these examples of how our model works out will help to clarify other issues as we go through this book, and perhaps in the reader's own experience it may help to clear up ideas which have been confusing, and even guilt-creating. Now, however, we must look at three common terms.

THE SPECTRUM

When the light of the sun shines through a prism, or through raindrops which act as a prism, we get the beautiful rainbow effect. All those beautiful colours are there in the light, yet thanks to the prism we see the whole SPECTRUM. We shall be using this illustration often in the coming pages, to describe the different levels of which we have been thinking; it indicates the wonderful unity of the human being, while at the same time it shows that there are different levels of our being.

Inevitably we use UP and DOWN to describe our spectrum in the "model", and we think of "spirit" as *higher*. Yet we must not think that "spiritual" is *better* than "physical". Each level has its appropriate place. For instance if Mother Teresa had opted for a "spiritual" approach to the poverty in Calcutta, and had stayed in her nunnery being spiritual and praying for the dying, that would have been a less Christly response than her very physical response to their needs. On the other hand, without a profound prayer life, the burden of human sin and suffering would have crushed her.

Therefore let us come back to the UNITY of the human being, indeed to the unity of humanity! **All that separates and sets one aspect against another is "not of God", who seeks to draw all things into unity (Ephesians 1:10), the unity of love, which gives everything and every one the proper place, and full value.**

ALTERED STATE OF CONSCIOUSNESS

This is the second expression which we are going to use frequently: ASC for short. There are many types of ASC, from very slightly heightened awareness to deep trance, meditation, hypnosis, resting in the Spirit (or being slain in the Spirit as some call it), out of the body experiences, and so on.

These states come in three ways:

* They come unsought, apparently in random fashion, at a time when one is concerned with something else.

* They come as the gift of God for a particular purpose.

* They can be deliberately induced by techniques developed by eastern gurus or by psychologists.

Let us look at each of these. Many of us have experienced such states unsought. Perhaps listening to music we slip into something like a meditation-state. A more extreme example is that of a lady I know whose car went out of control. She was watching it as it crashed down the mountain-side, thinking quite calmly: "My body is in that"... a very different state of consciousness! She woke up in the car, relatively unhurt.

Sometimes, however, it is God's special gift. I think of a man who was terrified of the operation which he was due. Being a Christian he prayed about his fear, and found himself carried away up into light, looking down on a small dark object. He asked, "What's that?" and the answer came, "That's the body you are so worried about". He woke up with no fear.

On the other hand these states can be manipulated, for they involve a change in the brain-wave pattern, switching to Alpha-waves. Therefore it is possible to learn to switch the pattern, and get oneself into an ASC. One can find many books which tell how to do this, but as in everything else human, some people find it easier to do than others. We should stress that those who find it easier are not necessarily superior, more spiritual or nearer God than those who cannot get an ASC to order.

In whatever way we move into an ASC, there is one thing that is common to them all: the rational, thinking mind is switched off, so to speak, and we are *aware* at a deeper level. However this "switching off" leaves us open to influences which we would not accept in our normal state. **Material hidden deep in our own sub-conscious may come to the surface and we may not know how to handle it.** There are unhealthy, unholy elements in our psychic environmemt, and with our defences down, we may "catch an infection".

Where the ASC is the direct work of the Holy Spirit, one can take it that there is no danger, but any deliberate creation of an ASC for oneself or for another calls for careful thought. **One's state of consciousness is something very sacred and precious. It has to be handled with great reverence and care.**

As a general rule then, we have to say that it is dangerous to seek an ASC for itself, for entertainment, for boosting your ego, or for escapism. If you are drawn to some form of ASC, be very careful of your motives. There are a number of cases of teenagers who experimented with ASC's, "just for a laugh", and ended up very disturbed people.

Even when we seek an ASC in a Christian setting, it can go wrong. Here are two examples:

RESTING IN THE SPIRIT*

Often in a healing service people will fall backwards, "resting in the Spirit". This is a lovely, healing experience, and many have been blessed through it. Yet one finds after a while that some people come to the service IN ORDER TO HAVE THE EXPERIENCE. What had begun by being Christ-centred, has subtly swung round to being self-centered, although the person would never acknowledge it. Once it is self-centred one is no longer protected in the way in which one is protected when an ASC is Christ-centred.

* See John Richards' booklet "Resting in the Spirit"

MEDITATION

People who have a deep, hidden hurt often become very agitated when they try to meditate, because, as we mentioned above, a deep hurt starts coming to the surface with which they cannot cope. Meditation should be confined to people who are part of a community or under the guidance of an experienced spiritual director, so that such elements can be dealt with. It should be part of one's total prayer-life. The actual techniques, however, are often available on the open market without such safeguards, and some people may find them helpful... if they are lucky!

ANASTHAESIA

There is another ASC which most of us face from time to time, although we do not recognize it as such: anaesthesia. We have all been grateful for anaesthetics at some time or other, but perhaps more work needs to be done on understanding what state of consciousness we ARE in when we have been given that "jag". Esmond Jefferies in his book *The Power and the Glory* tells of how he was dealing with a lady who had a terror of hospitals. Under hypnosis that woman was able repeat word for word the whole conversation which had gone on in the operating theatre on a previous occasion while she was supposed to be unconscious... it was enough to scare anybody! Perhaps we do not know enough about states of consciousness... or of UNconsciousness! Surely it is important to commit oneself to God, and claim protection while one is no longer in control of one's environment.

To sum up:

Since the integration of body-psyche-intellect-spirit is the aim in life, we have to be careful about separating them. Any deliberate entering into an ASC must be preceded by our being ruthlessly honest about our motives. It should always be in a setting in which we can be helped if things go wrong. And we should claim the protection of the Spirit (see Ephesians 6) before entering an ASC.

These two expressions, SPECTRUM, and ALTERED STATE OF CONSCIOUSNESS will be often used. Before we go any further, the third expression we need to look at is:

G-O-D

Some of you who read this may be quite sure that you know what the word means. That is good, and we rejoice for you. May your relationship with God go on deepening! Some of you who read this may be utterly confused as to what it means, and may have given up on the concept altogether. That is all right. You are on the verge of a great discovery!

For if God IS God, then obviously God is the Mind which created not just the universe which we see, but the unseen worlds beyond our senses. Such a being is obviously beyond us! Some of us have caught glimpses, and feel that we do in some way know God. But whenever we try to sum God up in some neat theory, or enclose God in some church or temple, we find eventually that it is left behind, empty.

What is one to make of those of us who think that we "know

God"... and may even have had some sort of vision of God?

We are like people who have paddled in a rock pool left behind by the tide, sailing our little boats on its waters, and thinking that we have seen the sea and know it. We may be very sure of our own little pools. Yet what does such a person know of the mighty Atlantic rollers as they thunder against the Orkney cliffs? Or of the long dark swell of the Pacific? Or of the depths in which strange creatures live?

In the same way some of us have paddled and sailed our little churchy boats in a rock-pool, and perhaps a shaft of sunlight did once break through and light up the pool with glory. It would be foolish either to belittle what experience we do have on the one hand or on the other to think that we know all the answers to life's mystery!

In one sense some of us have caught a glimpse of God, but it is also true that nobody has even seen God. As James Stephens says in *The Crock of Gold*:

> ....until there is a common eye no one person can see God, for the eye of all nature will scarcely be great enough to look upon that majesty. We shall greet happiness by multitudes, but we can greet HIM only by starry systems and a universal love.

Or, to look at it from another angle, perhaps you know the story of C.S.Lewis. His writings helped thousands, if not millions to find faith. Then his wife died, and in his book *A Grief Observed* he tells how he moved into "the dark night of the soul" when he who had explained it all so simply to others, found himself lost. "Found himself lost"? How can you find yourself and be lost at the same time? Yet that is just what happened to him. He had to lose the God he had explained so neatly, and confront the dark mystery behind all things, finding God and himself at a new level. So let us all, believer and unbeliever, start afresh.

ASKING THE RIGHT QUESTION

If you ask "Is there a God?" then the best answer is NO. But God IS. Puzzled? You can ask "Is there a Loch Ness monster?" or "Are there such things as fairies?" But if God is God, then he is not a thing lying around the universe somewhere, waiting for humans to discover or disprove it.

You will not find a God in the universe any more than you will find Sir Walter Scott in the Waverley Novels! But if you know Sir Walter Scott, you will see many traces of his character as you read the novels.

So we forget the "Is there a God?" question. It has been debated for centuries without any firm answer emerging. However we can and should ask: **"Does the universe, and human life in particular, have any meaning, and is there a purpose behind it all? Does life in some way respond to us?"** Then we are on the way.

MATERIALISTS

For the materialist, atheist, the answer to the above question is NO. They see the whole process as meaningless, just chance, and you make of it the best you can. Some follow this by living an utterly selfish life, but on the other hand some people have come to terms with such an idea and have lived noble lives. And many who claim to be Christian seem to feel deep down that there is nothing outside themselves to live for, whatever their surface beliefs.

PANTHEISTS

There are some who answer YES, and they see the process itself as being GOD. There is a strong element in eastern religions which takes this line, and many New Age people follow it. We call them PANTHEISTS, believing that "all is god". They see us as being part of a vast organism which is in the process of becoming....becoming what? That is the mystery.

One leading exponent of this line often begins his talks by saying something like this: "I have good news for you. You are not sinners". Since there is no objective God who loves, suffers and judges, there is no sin. What you do is part of the process, be it "good" or "bad" by normal standards. Strangely enough such people are often very concerned about the harm which humanity is doing to the environment, and that is very much what the Bible means as "sin"! However, as somebody said, perhaps "consistency is the mark of a small mind".

MONOTHEISTS

Then there are the MONOTHEISTS, "one God"-ists. They follow on from the Jewish tradition, the painful process traced out in the "Old Testament". Through the bloodshed, the darkness and the spiritual struggles there emerges the picture of a God who made all things and whose concern is that human beings should treat each other justly and care for this planet.

First of all Christianity and then Islam followed on from this, each offering a different development of what was in the Old Testament.

The big question in all these religions is: "How does God react to the fact that we humans do not treat each other justly and that we are doing terrible things to his Earth?"

The Jews came to terms with the problem through their temple and its sacrifices, until the Romans destroyed it. More recent Jewish prayers and writings show a deep awareness of God's mercy, and so do many of the Islamic writings.

Christians on the other hand see the conflict between human wrong and God's rightness focused on the Cross of Jesus. There are many ways of explaining what happened there at Calvary, and many people I know in the New Age movement have been put off Christianity because of what they THINK that Christians say... or perhaps by what some Christians DO say.

However, one can spend a lifetime always finding new depths of meaning in the mystery of the Cross. In the course of this book we shall refer to some of them. If we try to go into it at depth now, you will never get into the material with which this book is concerned! Suffice it to say that Christians believe that in Jesus we see God's own self-picture. We see the Father* suffering over his wayward children, in agony over the way we treat each other and the world. Yet we also see that the love of God rises above it all.

* God is not a HE, neither is God a SHE. Yet either of these is preferable to referring to God as an IT. The God who created personality cannot be less than personal, a mere impersonal IT. In biblical terms, humanity is referred to as being in the image of God before the male/female divide comes in. Jesus taught us to call God "ABBA"..."Father"; this is not the formal word which has been already used in this book. Those who have had problems with earthly fathers often find a problem in calling God "Abba", but they have all the more need to find a Father who is holy and loving. In this book we refer to God as HE, realising that we only do so because there is no better way! All human language is inadequate.

THREE-FOLD UNITY

In the Holy Spirit we see God at work in humanity, especially in those who have opened their lives in love to God so that they share with Jesus the awareness, "You are my beloved son/daughter in whom I delight".

This three-foldness is something we cannot get round.

Take away Jesus... and nobody would ever imagine that the Father is like that! Equally without the life of Jesus to consult, all sorts of strange things can be attributed to the Holy Spirit in us. Without the Cross, "God is Love" becomes sugary sentimentality. Without Jesus we are left with human attempts to describe that which cannot be described.

Take away the Holy Spirit... and you are left with a man 2,000 years ago and a Creator God, but nothing in us today. Without the Holy Spirit in us we are left with moral teaching which we always fail to live up to.

Take away the Father... and then Jesus and the Holy Spirit are signposts pointing to nowhere!

"God is LOVE" says the New Testament (the part of the Bible about Jesus).

* Love over all: *the Father*.

* Love penetrating the depths of Love's own creation: *Jesus*.

* Love lighting up our lives and our communities, shaping them in the Jesus-direction: *the Holy Spirit*.

The three are one. All three are love, and all love is one-ness.

Having written that, I know that it is totally inadequate to describe what I mean, or what anybody means by g-o-d. The deeper one's love for God, the more useless it is to try to find words to express it! That is true of human-human love, let alone human-God love!

RELIGIOUS PEOPLE

In all the religions to which we have referred, and within most Christian denominations you will find four main "wings". Each has its strengths and each has its weaknesses.

The *FUNDAMENTALISTS*: These are people who like things "cut and dried", "black and white". Their enthusiasm gives them a real strength, and they are very prominent. (Some Charismatics are fundamentalist, some are not. Some fundamentalists are Charismatic, many are very much against the Charismatic movement.)

The *FORMALISTS*: They observe their basic religious duties, try to keep a reasonably moral way of life, but distrust religious enthusiasm. They often seem to be the majority!

The *MYSTICS*: They move into expanding areas of awareness, both of God and of others. They have moved beyond the "cut and dried" approach.

30

The *ACTIVISTS*: They are not much concerned with theory and mystery, but rather they fling themselves wholeheartedly into some good cause.

Now no one person fits neatly into any of these categories. It is as if these are four points on the edge of a circle, and we are all moving about within that circle. In fact most of us who are spiritually alive have some experience of each of them in a lifetime. Whatever our character type, we have to learn to appreciate the other point of view.

I spell out these positions because many of the New Age people with whom I have spoken have been put off Christianity by what appears to them as bigotry in the fundamentalist line and also by what appears to be deadness in the formalists. Many such thinking people have never come across a reasonable statement of what the Gospel is. That is perhaps because they have never found it interesting enough to bother looking. One such person whom I met coming out of a service in Iona Abbey, slightly bewildered, commented sadly, "I know more about Hinduism and Buddhism than I do about Christianity".

On another occasion after I had spoken to 400 teachers of Yoga on the subject of Christian Meditation, many of them commented to me: "If we had only known there was this teaching in Christianity we would not be doing this!" Perhaps in reading this, as a by-product, some will begin to think it worthwhile giving another thought as to what Christianity really is.

THE TARGET: LOVE

Having tried to clarify what we mean, and do not mean, by G-o-d, we look at the most fundamental principle of all to guide us on our search. All the main religions would recognize the truth enshrined in Jesus' summary of the Law. The first command is: **You are to love the Lord your God with all your heart and soul and mind and strength.** The second is like it: **Love your neighbour as yourself.**

If we compare it with a target, then aiming at loving communion with God is the bull's eye, and the inner ring around it (the magpie) is love for others. If we are aiming at the bull's eye, with all-round love for others, then everything else will fall into place.

On the other hand anything can become evil if it has moved into the area which should be filled by God. This is especially dangerously so when in it is "religion" which moves into my sights. Few people do as much harm as those for whom their version of "the church" or of "the faith", has become central, and who see God and the church as their personal property. This is the real meaning of idolatry. Very few of us church folk have not fallen for this at times, especially when we thought that we were being truly dedicated! It was what brought the pharisees into enmity against Jesus.

Having looked at "religion" let us take four other examples of good things which can go wrong:

TRANSACTIONAL ANALYSIS (TA) has been a great help to many people as a way of understanding people... and self! Jean Morrison in her book about TA calls it "A TOOL FOR CHRISTIANS", although of course non-Christians find it helpful too. It may help us to steady our aim and to get love for others clearer. But if it moves too near to the centre, and we begin to think that it has all the answers, it becomes an obsession.

PSYCHIC PHENOMENA are part of life and are fascinating, but all the great spiritual teachers in all religions warn their disciples against becoming preoccupied with them. They happen, they may appear helpful, but they must never become the main aim. They are so interesting, so ego-boosting that they present a real temptation, but they must be kept in their right place. God, by whatever name God is known, must always be the aim, and that is the high teaching of all religion.

MORALITY AND JUSTICE come very near the bull's eye, yet even here, if people become preoccupied with them and lose that focal LOVE FOR GOD from their sights, legalism corrupts morality and people are then sacrificed to policies and principles.

HEALTH AND WHOLENESS are precious, and it is is good and natural to seek them. However if I begin to think that the God and the church are there to help ME to fulfill MYSELF, and that the object of prayer is to get MY will done, then I am away off target! We know too that pre-occupation with MY health is very unhealthy!

There are other examples of things which are good in themselves but yet become destructive through being turned into an "idol". However, part of life's process is trying out many aims, getting many different targets in view. One after the other turns out not to have been the target at which we were meant to be aiming, or else, having reached it, we find that it has to be left behind.

So we go on seeking, until at last we get it right, and with the old Irish saint can sing, and mean, BE THOU MY VISION, O LORD OF MY HEART.

Finally we come to this basic rule:

When considering the rightness or the wrongness of any activity, we must not look at it in isolation, but consider its rightful setting in a properly targeted life.

4 SUMMING UP SO FAR

Now let us draw together some of these guidelines. Perhaps one could use these for group discussion. In any case, check them with your own experience.

* Good and evil, like God, meet us at every level of our being.

* Since the integration of body-psyche-intellect-spirit is the aim in life, we have to be careful about separating them.

* Any deliberate entering into an ASC must be preceded by our being ruthlessly honest about our motives, and in a setting in which we can be helped if things go wrong.

* Like attracts like.

* The deeper one goes into the psychic and spiritual spheres the greater the effect on others at a level below consciousness.

* If a person is truly focused upon God in faith and in love, then such psychic elements as are needed for the Lord's work will be given.

* A person who deliberately develops psychic sensitivity is in real danger.

* The higher up the spectrum, the more critical the issues.

* When considering the rightness or the wrongness of any activity, we must not look at it in isolation, but consider its rightful place in a properly targeted life.

* God is the ultimate mystery, and we must never think that we have God summed up and confined to any human words or institutions.

* We may say "GOD IS LOVE", but a life-time is not long enough to discover what that means.

* The Life of Jesus expresses that mystery which we call God, and is the point at which we can begin to know God. We can spend a lifetime exploring that Life: it is never neatly contained in somebody's theology.

Part II: THE BIBLICAL TEXTS

Having sharpened up the word-tools we shall be using, we are going to head straight for the dividing line between the two movements we started with, examining the Bible text in detail.

5 FORBIDDEN AREAS?

Long centuries before Jesus (scholars differ on how many) a collection of Jewish rules and regulations was compiled, and we call it DEUTERONOMY, which means "the second law". We are going to look at chapter 18, verses 10 and 11. Books from the Charismatic Christian side attacking the New Age movement always quote these as key verses, so if we look at them, we shall soon find that the vital issues are confronting us.

Verse 10 appears among a whole lot of Do's and Don't's which relate to how the life of God's People must be different from the life of the surrounding nations. We have first to ask whether these rules given to Israel many centuries BC (before Christ) really apply, as many modern Christian books suggest, to what we know today as homoeopathy, astrology, ESP research, spiritualism, and much else which is included under the title 'New Age'.

Let us look, then at how these verses, orginally in Hebrew, are translated into English - first the REVISED STANDARD VERSION (RSV) **There shall not be found among you any one who burns his son or his daughter as an offering, any one who practises divination, a soothsayer, or an augur, or a sorcerer, or a charmer, or a medium, or a wizard, or a necromancer.**

Now the JERUSALEM BIBLE (JB - the Roman Catholic translation): **There must never be anyone among you who makes his son or daughter pass through the fire, who practices divination, who is a soothsayer, augur or sorcerer, who uses charms, consults ghosts or spirits, or calls up the dead.**

We can find plenty of references to these individual practices in other parts of the Bible*, but nowhere else is it so clearly put, with all the forbidden areas together in one place. No wonder that this is a favourite text to quote.

To the average reader the meaning is crystal clear, and it is quite enough of a warning sign for most people, but to the person who has been finding the way from a secular culture towards a spiritual one via the New Age movement it begs the question. For those who have no biblical background, and no affiliation to any one religion, the Bible appears as just another old book... interesting perhaps, in parts. But just quoting a text like this at them is more likely to put them off reading further than to invite them to explore more deeply.

The more thoughtful would go on to ask if the person quoting these verses takes all the commands in the Bible literally. For instance what about the frequent attacks on charging interest? Or about the redistribution of land every 49 years? It turns out that even the most literal-minded fundamentalist finds a way round some of the commands!

Are these translations of the Hebrew words accurate? What are the fundamental principles which can guide us through such an exploration?

*Further references are in Leviticus 19:31 and 20:6,27. Leviticus is a book of regulations for the Jewish people defining how they are to be different from the nations around them. Also Isaiah 7:16-19, 47:12-15, Jeremiah 7:16-19 (amid protests against a corrupt, unjust society).

THROUGH THE FIRE

The first thing forbidden involves fire. The RSV refers to sacrificing children, the JB to making them pass through the fire. One would think that it was hardly worth spending time looking at this, for who would want to do that today anyway?

Wait a moment, though. In an article in the Scots Magazine (May 1988) Rennie McOwan tells how even into the last century young people had a "passing through" fire ritual up on Ben Ledi at "Beltane". A century before that, in Iona, the cattle were still driven round *Cnoc nan Aingheal* through fire at Beltane. So it is not all that long-forgotten a practice. The idea of calling up the elemental spirits to protect cattle and children etc. still lingers in folk-memory. Furthermore there was on TV not long ago a programme about an American teaching fire-walking. So we cannot really forget about this.

What lies behind it? We have already hinted at it. The old belief was that there were the basic elements of earth and air, fire and water. Each had its DEMONS; this word did not originally mean something evil, it links with the word *deva* in India which we usually translate "god" (with a small g). When the New Testament refers to people having an evil spirit, the actual Greek original says "he had an unclean demon". (It never says that they were "possessed" by a demon, it is always the other way round.) The fact that they feel they have to say that it was an UNCLEAN demon, shows that demons were not always unclean.

We shall have to look in more detail at this later, but in the meantime, let us see that what was being forbidden was dedicating your children to the fire demons. The People of God are to deal direct with the Living God, not with the elemental demons. However, now that so few children are baptized into the Family of God, it is very likely that soon one will hear of children "passing through the fire" again, for this is the strange thing that is happening today: as Christian rituals are rejected, people are reverting to the very things from which our forefathers were glad to be delivered.

The Bible does refer to such beings (e.g. Ephesians 1:21 & 3:10-11... and see further in chapter 11), but it warns us against tangling with them*. If one reads some of the stories about these beings in their old versions, not in their idealized Victorian form, one finds how continually people who call up these powers for help get more than they bargain for. As for opening a gate into a child's life through which such forces can operate, well... it is asking for trouble, when one should be opening the gate into the Love of God. Perhaps it was the best they could do once, but for us the higher thing is available, and there should be no question of reverting to the old. On the other hand, perhaps we should take infant baptism more seriously.

* An amusing example of this is the story of a harvest at the north end of Iona. It was a heavy harvest and the farmer was worried as to how he was going to get it in. A *bodachan*, a little old man, offered to help, asking only as much of the harvest as he could tie in his belt. The farmer accepted the offer, and the little old man out-did all the other harvesters with his heuk. When all was cut, he laid out his belt and began to load the crop on. As he did so the belt grew and grew until he had the whole crop. Thereupon he tied it up and vanished with the lot! You may doubt the historicity of the story, but the moral is clear: think twice before you enlist the help of the *sidh*.

DIVINATION

The next "forbidden area" in Deut 18:10 is divination, and this is the translation in all the versions. That leaves us with the question: "What is divination"?

The Hebrew word is *qesem*, and it means 'throwing'. It refers to the old practice of throwing cards, arrows, dice etc. in order to make up your mind what you should do. In Ezekiel 21:21 for instance, it refers to the Babylonian king having thrown arrows in order to decide which way his army should march, and therefore which city he should attack.

This practice depends on the belief that if you open the situation to "chance" then the "gods" can guide you. This method of decision-making is what is forbidden. If the way the arrows fall, or the way the cards in the tarot pack fall, is in fact controlled by some unseen intelligence, what is that intelligence? If such forces exist, how do we know that they are beneficent? How do we know that their aims are the same as ours? If we read the stories which the ancients tell about their "gods" we find that these "gods" were very caught up in a lot of nasty in-fighting among themselves, and consequently invoking one of them was liable involve you in their squabbles.

One may of course say, "Chance is chance, and that is all there is to it". In which case it remains a poor, immature way of making a decision. On the other hand if you say: "There is no such thing as chance", and you believe that some other intelligence does operate this way, then there are a lot of questions to be asked.

Therefore, whichever way you look at it, the reason is apparent why the People of God are not to shape their political, military and personal decisons by "chance". They are to consult the prophets of the Living God, and to seek his Will. When Deuteronomy was written there was not a "Bible" as we know it, so they could not be told to consult the Bible, however for us today the way to make decisions is through study of the Bible and through prayer, both individual and corporate, using our intelligence and acting responsibly. Since, as Deut 6:5 says, the main thing in human life is to love the Lord our God with heart and soul and strength (at all levels of our being), we are not to be subject to lower forces, assuming that such exist.

WAIT A MOMENT!

That is all very well, but what about a football match? We toss up to decide which end we'll take... is that breaking God's Law?

Such an apparently frivolous question brings us to an important point: the referee is not seeking the guidance of God or of any other entity, he is not opening the situation to any outside intelligence, what might be called "the supernatural element" is missing, so it does not come under the heading of *qesem* even though it is "throwing".

What is forbidden, then is a coming-together of three elements:

* Decision-making

* The element of chance

* Seeking guidance elsewhere than from the Living God

This brings us to an important principle which will apply to many of the items which follow:

It is not the physical action which is condemned, but subjecting oneself to beings other than the Lord our God.

BUT WHAT ABOUT...

Yes, but what about the Urim and the Thumim, part of the priest's regalia in the Bible, carried in a pouch on his chest, and used to ascertain God's Will by throwing? Strangely, here we find a *qesem* not forbidden but actually authorized! Even stranger is the fact that no examples are given of its use. One is left with the feeling that it cannot have been very important to them.

Far more puzzling is the fact that in Acts 1:26 we read that the apostles cast lots to decide which man was to fill the vacancy in the Twelve. Here we have the apostles using a *qesem*!

Yet this illustrates precisely the principle stated: in the case of the priests using the Urim and Thumim and the apostles casting lots, it was the Will of God which was sought. It is not so much the action but the source of guidance which is sought that matters.

So should we resort to methods of decision-making which involve chance? From a purely materialistic point of view, it is a very immature way of going about things as a rule. However, the more you believe that there are unseen forces at work through chance, the more careful you have to be. For instance people quote strange things happening when they use the tarot pack for decison-making, on the assumption that the power they have invoked is good. Yet many have landed themselves in darkness through this, and have needed to find deliverance.

THE RANDOM VERSE

We can hardly pass from this without looking at one experience which many of us had: opening the Bible at random and finding God's guidance in the verse before us. This is not "throwing", but it is very like it. The main books on prayer all advise against using this technique, although God does seem to use it, especially for beginners. It very easily becomes just a superstitious use of the Bible, replacing mature study and prayer.

We come back, then to something fundamental:
We grow in love for God and for others, by learning to make responsible decisions. In Roman 12:2, we read that we find out what God wants us to do, as our minds are renewed by the Holy Spirit. That is how we should make decisions. We should therefore not use "chance" in our decision-making.

Too great a dependence on "signs" and on special guidance, even in a Christian context, is a mark of immaturity, an evading of responsibility, but we recognise that on occasion God does use a sign of some sort to guide us in circumstances where we ourselves could not arrive at the decision needed. (See further in chapter 13)

Summing up this section we must notice another basic principle:
When quoting the Bible, one cannot always equate the modern English words and their meaning with what the Hebrew original said. Disciplined study is needed.

DOWSING

Because *qesem* was translated as "divination", and because we talk about "water divining" and such-like, people apply this prohibition to activities which have nothing to do with "throwing".

Take an example: I knew an old man who saved the local authorities thousands of pounds because if they ever lost track of a gas main or a water main, they would send for him. Then, instead of the costly and inconvenient way of digging exploratory trenches to find them, he would get a metal coat-hanger, bend it and trace the line of the lost pipe.

One person said to me: "That should be stopped, it's divination, it's of the devil". We have to ask, however, is it in fact *qesem*? There is no question of throwing, of chance, and certainly the old man never thought of it as getting guidance from anything supernatural... he thought of it as something to do with electro-magnetism.

Applying the principles we looked at in the previous section, we have to conclude that whatever may be banned under *qesem*, so-called water-divining is not. It is better to use the term DOWSING, and tackle the issues without referring to *qesem*.

We can get a better idea of what dowsing is if we look at an excerpt from a centre which teaches it among other "alternative medicine" techniques:

> Dowsing or divining, is a non-intrusive method, without side-effects, of finding the sources of problems and selecting suitable remedies for humans animals, plant-life and the earth. Tracing faults in power-cables, water pipes, reservoirs, gas pipes, lines of earth energy, finding missing objects, checking food qualities etc. are practical applications of this faculty.

IS IT OCCULT?

The word occult means HIDDEN, and it refers to hidden or secret knowledge which gives the person who knows power over other things and over people.

Now we have to face the fact that much that we take for granted would have been thought "occult" a few generations ago. In fact many primitive people do not distinguish between the "white man's magic" and their own medicine man's magic. It is all occult to them. If somebody had invented electrical gadgets three centuries ago, he would have been liable to be burned for witchcraft. We have to be careful about using this word.

Just because we do not understand something, it is not necessarily "occult" in our modern meaning of the word. If dowsing is to do with electro-magnetism then a future generation may take it for granted, just as we take it for granted that when we press a switch, the light will come on.

Now another step: the word "occult" is usually taken to refer to knowledge which is deliberately kept secret in order to boost the ego of the person who knows. Now this is not the case in water-dowsing. That old man was keen to show others and to get them to do it too, and just recently in a agricultural show I saw a notice inviting people to learn "water- divining". There is not much "hidden" there!

It seems doubtful, therefore, whether this activity can really be labelled "occult". In fact in some parts of the world people depend on it for their very lives. If it is a necessary art for survival, surely it cannot be always "of the devil".

On the other hand, there IS a psychic element in it. For instance in dowsing one has to concentrate on the object to be found. If the old man had let his mind wander on to WATER when he was supposed to be looking for GAS, the result might have been disastrous! So we see that even if it is a physical thing such as electro-magnetism, it involves the psyche as well, so we have moved up the spectrum, and therefore must be a bit more careful.

Yet we have to ask those who condemn it: since this is a very real bit of public service, and in some cases a matter of life and death, can those who would condemn it as diabolic offer an alternative? Bushmen in the Kalahari can hardly be expected to carry round with them expensive apparatus to make test-bores for water... so what would the person who considers dowsing diabolic suggest? Or to take another example: if the above local authority had approached the group of Christians who condemned this activity, would the latter, under the guidance of the Holy Spirit have been able to offer the same public service?

Yet another question arises. Are there people who are completely Christ-centred who help people this way? I do not know the answer. While it can be used in association with "other gods", and thus in forbidden ways, is there possibly a right use of this technique? The old man with whom we began seemed to have no particular religious affiliations.

And here is another question: Can anybody do it? A friend of mine was working on a highland estate. If they needed to track a drain or some such, there was one man in the squad who would just cut a twig and trace it out for them. My friend, a strong Christian, often tried it but it never worked for him, but if the other man held his elbow, the twig would bend in the appropriate way. So it would seem that as with many other things in life, some can do it and some cannot. It is those who CAN who can learn more and develop the gift.

While much needs to be thought through*, we can at least say that there is nothing unbiblical about dowsing, it is not really occult, and that many who condemn it do so on inadequate grounds. They may or may not be right so to condemn it, but the grounds which I have seen given for doing so do not convince me that it is wrong in itself. However, if anybody tries to use it to get information to which they are not entitled, then it would be evil indeed. That is a real temptation.

*It should be easy to check the accuracy of dowsing, yet many will remember a programme on TV in which a number of well-known dowsers all failed to locate their quarry. Samuel Pfeifer in *Healing at any price?* quotes an experiment in New Zealand with 75 dowsers - the results could have been obtained by guessing; he also

42

tells how in Switzerland 16 famous dowsers including 11 engineers and a professor, were sent to 7 fields to locate underground water pipes. They completely failed, even though one pipe was carrying 4,000 gallons a minute! In several other places they claimed to have located pipes when there were none! Perhaps such tests are in conditions which make concentration hard, but they certainly make one chary of individual, anecdotal claims.

CLUSTERS

Before we leave our dowsing friend there are two more points to make:

Firstly, as we have noted already, his dowsing for mains seemed to be just one of his interests, unconnected with anything else. In the same way as A repairs cars for people (a very occult area for me!) and B makes good wine, so this man dowsed for the council... just a hobby that was useful to the community.

However in many cases dowsing is only part of a cluster of interests. It is often part of an unhealthy pre-occupation with the supernatural, the para-normal. Then one thing leads to another and before long the person is involved with much at the psychic level without having the spiritual awareness that is needed to cope with it. Mistaking these things for "spiritual", people get "hooked" on them, and they become unhealthy.

This leads us to see that something such as dowsing, and many of the other things at which we will be looking, may be harmless in themselves, but dangerous as part of a "cluster". We have already noted that *qesem* is accepted without comment in Acts 1 as part of the "cluster" of Biblical things, but forbidden as part of the "cluster" of practices which went with Canaanite religion.

We shall therefore have to look carefully at a number of the items which follow, asking whether they are wrong *in themselves*, or whether they are suspect because they are usually found in unhealthy clusters of interest. We could re-phrase a question we asked earlier about *qesem*: is the use of chance permissible as part of a cluster of Christian devotion, but not in other clusters?

This will be especially important when we consider healing techniques, for so often an apparently harmless and possibly helpful technique turns out to be only the first step into all sorts of strange things.

In judging the rightness or wrongness of any activity, look not only at the activity itself, but at the cluster of which it is a part.

THE EGO-TRIP

The second point before we leave the old dowser is that his attitude to it was a very healthy one. He took a rightful pride in being able to help people this way, but he did not seem to think that he was better than others for being able to do so. There is a proper pride in being able to make an engine run sweetly, or in making a wine which pleases friends, but these can easily become distorted into becoming what we call an EGO-TRIP... something which is done only to boost one's ego.

As we noted earlier, the higher up the spectrum, the more careful one has to be about this. The man who has made engine-repair into an ego-trip is just a bore, whereas the preacher who has made his pulpit performance into an ego-trip is really a menace. The singer who joins the church choir just in order to show off her singing is equally turning worship into an ego-trip, and will cause much trouble in the church. In the Charismatic movement we know only too well the trouble caused by people who have allowed "their gift of prophecy" to become a weekly ego-trip, threatening to bring the whole movement into disrepute.

Coming back to dowsing, we have to ask questions about motivation, noting that it seems to be moving into the psychic band in the spectrum, and therefore one has to be that bit more careful about one's motives than in the case of the man who repairs engines.

Here again we have stumbled on an important principle which will serve us well as the book unfolds:

Anything good can become an ego-trip, and the higher up the spectrum, the more dangerous it is. Conversely, because something tempts people into an ego-trip, it is not necessarily wrong in itself.

PENDULUMS

Now let us look at a specific area of dowsing which is very popular with New Age people: **Using a pendulum for medical diagnosis**.

To illustrate the problem: a friend was visiting a lady, who, when my friend mentioned a back-problem, immediately said: "I think I can help." She then produced a pendulum. My friend immediately said: "No thank you".

"Why not? I've helped a lot of people this way."

"I'm a Christian", my friend replied.

"But so am I. What's wrong with a pendulum?"

The only reason my friend could give was that she had read in various

44

books that pendulums were of the devil. This of course is a very unsatisfactory answer, for the next question is: "Why do the books say that, and on what authority?"

It is a method which has helped so many people that we have to be very clear in our reasons before we write it off as diabolic along with ouija boards. Let us seek this clarity now.

THEIR USE

Talking to people with experience of this, it is quite clear that the pendulum is only properly used to ascertain facts. A number of people experienced in its use have emphasised to me that the pendulum should never be used in decision-making, for this should be done on moral and spiritual grounds. This is not a *qesem* then, although in a number of books this Biblical verse is quoted as the authority for condemning it. There is no question of anything random, but on the contrary, a considerable amount of medical knowledge and discipline is required, as we shall see.

How does it work? Practitioners have their own variations and short-cuts, but as a rule one begins by holding the pendulum still and asking "What is my positive sign?" It will move backwards and forwards perhaps. Then: "What is my negative sign?" and it might move sideways.

Having established that, one would hold the pendulum over one part of the patient's body asking, "Is the trouble here?" If the answer were negative one would move on to another part. Having located the trouble one would then ask: "Is it such and such a disease?" One might then hold it over a list of medicines or treatments until one got a positive sign.

Naturally, experienced practitioners, as we have noted, have their own ways, but this gives us something to work on. It will be obvious that the use of the pendulum involves quite a considerable knowledge of anatomy and medicine. In fact most doctors who use it always cross-check with conventional medical knowledge. Even then it can go wrong: I know of one case in which a doctor using a pendulum could find nothing wrong with a lady who went to him, and declared her pregnancy normal. Just in time she went to another doctor who spotted a serious condition... the first doctor had overlooked to ask "Is it ...?". That illustrates the danger in inadequate medical disciplines, and is a warning to amateurs.

It may help if we have an example of how this treatment works. A lady I know was told that her daughter was developing spinal arthritis, a serious complaint in a child. She phoned somebody who diagnosed by pendulum, and, still on the phone, he diagnosed that a certain vertebra had been displaced: "Has she been playing hockey?" She had, and was duly taken to an osteopath, who set the spine back in position, and there was no more trouble with that. If the original medical diagnosis had been accepted, one dreads to think of the years of treatment that would have followed. This illustrates how simple and rapid diagnosis can be by this method if used by a properly qualified person.

In modern medicine diagnosis is becoming increasingly impersonal and costly. Highly complex diagnostic machines are installed in the major hospitals, and if one is an ordinary person, living in a housing scheme on the outskirts of the city, or in the country, getting to hospital may involve costly bus journeys, and is a generally frightening experience. On the other hand if such a simple diagnostic technique worked, and its results were cross-checked, it would save so much time and money... let alone sparing the sufferer the ordeal!

THE QUESTION: WHAT IS THE SOURCE OF THE INTELLIGENCE?

Most Christian doctors have experienced occasionally a flash of insight into a case which they feel was guidance by the Holy Spirit... in fact many doctors who would not claim to be Christian would say the same. However one would need to ask whether "the Gift of Knowledge" is known to give doctors the specific diagnosis in ordinary cases day by day, in a way that compares favourably with those who use a pendulum. That is a question for doctors... especially for Christian doctors.

Yet in every book I have read on the Charismatic side, pendulums are condemned as diabolic, so we will have to look at this. First of all we note that the grounds on which they are condemned is the verse in Deuteronomy 18... it is "divination" they say. But as we have seen, it is not *qesem*, for it is not decision-making, it is not chance... but there remains the question as to where the information comes from.

Somehow information is conveyed to the practitioner which is not available to his normal intellect. Or to put it another way: the pendulum is the way in which someone or something conveys information to the mind of the practitioner. But what is the source of this knowledge? Where does it come from? We seem to have moved into contacting something far more specific than could be explained by electro-magnetism as we thought with our dowser. Asking various practitioners one gets very different answers: "the Holy Spirit", "a high spirit", "a doctor who died early this century", "my higher self contacting the higher self of the patient", and so on. One is left asking still more questions.

WHERE DOES IT COME IN THE SPECTRUM?

As in all cases of dowsing, it requires a special sort of concentration, coming only with a lot of practice and discipline. Although the experienced can slip into it in seconds, it is an ASC. It is therefore an opening of the self to something or someone else... and we have seen already that this is dangerous. To God alone should we open our inner selves like this, and any confused thinking here can be fatal. It comes back to what we said earlier, that to develop aspects at the psychic level which one is not spiritually equipped to handle is asking for trouble. For instance those who are seeking an ego-trip to get the reputation of being a healer will attract unhealthy elements in the psychic environment. Such people may get some good results, but they will scatter infection like a doctor with a cold!

That leaves us with the question as to whether God could use this method to guide the doctor in the surgery... Thomas Haberle, a Benedictine monk seems quite sure that this is the case and he quotes many cases in which he has used the pendulum to help people (*Helping and Healing*, Sheldon Press).

However over years of experience in the Christian Fellowship of Healing we had experience of many Christian people who had thought that they were going to serve the Lord this way, and who came to grief. Having learned to use the pendulum, they found that their personal relationship with Jesus was getting dimmer and dimmer, and finally had to ask us to set them free from the pendulum. In one case it was several weeks later that we found that on the very afternoon we had delivered the person from the pendulum, somebody he had treated 40 miles away felt something like a black cloud lift. On another occasion a charming lady came into our Bible study, and made some good contributions to the discussion. Yet two of us sensed something dark. Later when we were about to pray with her for the relief of unexplained pain, we asked: "Do you believe that the Lord can do this for you?" She replied: "Of course, I'm a healer myself... look here's my little pendulum..."

We could quote many other examples of people who learned to use the pendulum, and later regretted it. Yet I have to admit that each of these seemed to have a personality problem, and was seeking to compensate for this by becoming "a healer". Looking back, they should never have been taught to use the pendulum or been engaged in "healing".

A conversation....

"Jesus did not use a pendulum, neither should we."
"Jesus did not use a stethoscope, or X-rays, yet we think it right for doctors to do so."
"We have the guidance of the Holy Spirit."
"Does the Holy Spirit not guide doctors too as they diagnose illness?"
"I feel it would be wrong for me to begin using anything like that."
"Quite rightly so. You are called to work at the level of the spirit. It would be wrong for you to use any form which belonged to the medical level. The question under discussion is whether the pendulum is a proper way of diagnosis for those who heal at the physical level, be they christian or non-christian."

CONCLUSION

There is nothing in the Bible which directly forbids the use of the pendulum in diagnosis. There is however a very definite principle: **we must not let ourselves be "controlled" by any power other than the Lord Himself.**

People, with the best of intentions, may try to short-cut this by opening themselves to lower powers, and even get good results in some cases, but they will spread "psychic infection". Therefore we must beware of allowing people to use the pendulum on us. Just because a person CLAIMS to be God-guided, it does not mean that this is the case.

Admitting that there is a wrong use of the pendulum, we are left asking whether there is a right use, under the guidance of the Holy Spirit. This is not a very satisfactory conclusion, and we have not arrived at that clarity which we set out to seek, but we warned the reader at the begining that some topics need a lot more work done on them.

6 READING THE SIGNS

AUGURY

The next word, *anan*, refers to clouds, and it would seem to refer to reading omens in the sky. The way the sentence in Deuteronomy runs, the two things "divination and augury" seem to hang together. As "casting" was a way of getting supernatural help in decision-making, so was augury.

We know, of course, that people have sought omens and guidance in the sky in all religions. The shape of the clouds, the way birds fly, the way the stars are set, are all favourite ways of finding out the best time for weddings, war, business and so on. Reading the old Celtic stories, one is struck by how often the flight of a bird is taken as "guidance". In Babylon they traced the signs of their gods in the sky, hence "the zodiac" and so on.

There seems to be a deep human feeling that there is a pattern behind things somewhere if only one could trace it. There is the universal "hunch" that there must be meaning in it all, if only one could find the secret key which would enable us to read it. Most of us have had experiences which have led us to say: "That is more than coincidence!" From that we begin to look for patterns in our surroundings. Some people claim to have the clue which enables them to read the riddle, and it is these who are referred to in this text.

JUST CHANCE?

We live in an age when most people have accepted what they think is a scientific view: that the whole universe is the result of chance, without meaning or purpose. Sensitive souls rebel against this, sure that there IS meaning and purpose, and they seek to grasp it. Hence the renewed interest in old ideas of how the pattern is to be discerned. This is to some extent a judgment on the Church for failing to speak clearly on these things, and consequently we find many attempts to fill in the gap, from astrologers on one hand to Jehovah's Witnesses on the other.

What the Bible stresses is that there is a Living God who will guide and shield his people, and that our concentration should be on our communion with him, not on trying to find somebody who can read the clouds etc. As a matter of fact, when we do enter into a closer communion with God, we do discern pattern and meaning in all sorts of places. But then we are no longer interested in finding the most propitious moment for our own undertakings, or in getting a prediction which will enable us to avoid trouble, but rather we become concerned to do His Will, even if it may mean "bad luck" from the human point of view. Jesus in the Garden of Gethsemane is the prime example of that.

For the nations who surrounded Israel, the object of "religion" was to get the gods to give good harvests and victories in battle. One had to know both how to avoid offending the gods, and how to please them with sacrifices. What Israel was being taught in passages such as the one we are looking at, is that God is concerned with justice and fair-dealing. God's agenda is about how people relate to one another. Prosperity and peace are the by-products of this, not items to be bought by sacrifices and through occult knowledge. In passages such as Isaiah 1 or Amos 5 the prophets, in God's Name, pour contempt on all the religious business, including rites commanded elsewhere in the Bible, stressing that what God wants is justice for the poor and for the underprivileged. People then, as now, prefer gods who are interested in religion and in "good luck"... they are so much more comfortable to live with than the God who identifies with the poor and the outcast! Or are they?

What, therefore, is forbidden here is consulting people with supposed secret knowledge as to how to get "good luck". This is not the way that a child of God should tackle life's problems.

ASTROLOGY

Let us suppose that astrology *does* come under the heading of *anan*, and look at it now.

We find astrologers mentioned fairly often in the Bible, as we saw in a previous footnote, grouped along with other "forbidden areas". Astrologers are held up to ridicule in Daniel, yet Magi are apparently led to the Christ-child partly by astrology! We have to be careful before we play the trump card: "The Bible says..."! This is an area of strong conflict between New Age and Charismatic Christians, and so we shall have to tread carefully, for Charismatics consider astrology to be Satanic.

WHAT IS ASTROLOGY?

Popular astrology is concerned, as were the ancients, with fortune-telling, with decision-making: deciding when to make a journey, start a war, get married and so on. Those who allow this to govern their lives are liable to form a real bondage to it. Serious students of astrology, however, despise popular astrology as it appears in the gutter press. The New Age concern with astrology is mainly about helping people to understand their basic make-up, and about medical treatment.

Their understanding is based on the belief that everything in the universe is inter-related and inter-dependent, and that therefore the position of the universe at the moment of birth and throughout our lives has a profound effect upon us. If it is a case of magnetic fields affecting us, then this is a matter of scientific investigation, and can be either proved or disproved. On the other hand if it is claimed that what is affected is something "higher up the spectrum", this is not proved or disproved so easily. For instance one astrologer claimed that a high proportion of successful athletes were born under a certain sign, but when others took random samples of successful athletes, they could find no such correlation. Such claims and counter-claims have not really helped to establish whether the effect of stars on character is a fact or not*. One comes back to anecdotal evidence: and one of such now follows.

*In January 1989 the Observer published an interesting supplement on Astrology. It quoted an experiment in France. In the French press on 16 April 1968 there was an advertisement offering free character profiles, asking people to send in their times and places of birth. Hundreds responded and duly received a profile. Many wrote back saying how accurate it was and how helpful it had been. What they did not know was that each person had been sent the same profile! It was the profile of a man born on January 17 1897. The leading French astrologer had been given only the birth-date, sex and place of birth of *this* man and had made up *his* chart. The man had turned out to be one of France's major war criminals!

The same supplement also had articles by leading journalists who were asked to take their horoscopes seriously for a month. The result was readable, hilarious, but hardly likely to impress one with a desire to do the same!

One could continue quoting example for and against, without ever coming to a firm conclusion. In the end you believe what you want to believe.

THE TWINS

To be personal for a moment, I have twin daughters, and one could not find two people less alike. Surely if two people so utterly different could be "born under the same sign", one could not deduce much about their characters because they share the same "sign".

When I put this to an experienced astrologer, she explained that in the few minutes between their births very vital changes could have taken place in the zodiac. Yet if such a change can happen in a matter of minutes, what is the point of saying that people under a certain sign have certain characteristics? It seems a "heads I win, tails you lose" situation. It would also mean that if one did not know the time of one's birth, then astrology would not help much.

On the other hand when one of these twins consulted a serious astrologer for a character chart, the result was quite wrong. The astrologer was puzzled, knowing that it was not like her customer at all. What she did not know was that she had described the character of the other twin, whom she had not met. On cross-checking, they found that the twin who had asked for the chart had given her sister's time of birth! (Incidentally, they found the charts very helpful in coming to terms with themselves.)

We are left with the feeling: "There must be something in it, but what?" Charismatics would say that it is a devilish deception, and that the way to understand one's nature is to open oneself to the Holy Spirit, not to an astrologer. Yet some Charismatics show a remarkable lack of self-knowledge!

Such an attempt to come to terms with one's nature, in order to be a better person, is not what the forbidden *anan* was about. Serious modern astrology is not about decision-making. It is concerned with understanding oneself and others. Such understanding can be used for good or bad. It may be used to create an excuse for weaknesses, forgetting that "the fault lies not in our stars but in ourselves". Each new understanding faces us with an option and that is the crucial point. The situation would be parallel to knowing one's family background: a help to come to terms with inherited strengths and weaknesses, but by no means a dominating factor in one's earthly pilgrimage. And if one does not know one's family background or one's time of birth, one may still enter into a full way of living, by the Grace of God.

In the meantime, when one hears people saying: "George seems to be bad-tempered these days, but he's a Leo, and it's a bad patch for Leos, so we'll make allowances for him until it is over", we are not dealing with that activity which is condemned in our text-verses, even if these do refer to astrology. Taking verses which refer to fortune-telling by the stars, and applying them to the attempt to understand character is not valid logic. We must dig deeper.

MACROCOSM & MICROCOSM

Gordon Strachan in his book *Christ and the Cosmos* looks at the whole mathematical structure of the created order, and how everything is inter-related and meaningful. One may or may not understand such mathematics, and few of us are in a position to judge whether he is right or wrong, yet if there are patterns which run through the macrocosm (the very great) and the microcosm (the very small) it is part of our duty as children of God to understand our Father's world, and to appreciate these wonderful patterns. What is evil, is to use the power this gives us for wrong ends.

In Colossians 1:17 we find the phrase "by him all things consist". In other words everything holds together in Christ. In Ephesians 1:10 we find that the purpose of God is to reconcile every*thing*(not every*one* only!) through Christ. In Romans 8:19-22 we have the picture of the whole created order joining in the struggle to produce the children of God, in fact it is pictured struggling and groaning, waiting and longing for us to come into our own, just as a mother struggles to produce her baby! All this presents us with the picture of a creation which is far more than a disposable back-drop to the little drama of "how I was saved and went to heaven". The creation is an active participant in the drama of life, not mere scenery!

Unfortunately the church has done little thinking on this line. Hymns such as *All things bright and beautiful* or *How great Thou art* do indeed speak to us of God in THE BEAUTY of nature, but they ignore "all things dark and terrible", and watching a few nature programmes on the TV leaves us with a a lot of questions if we have based our theology of nature on hymns such as these alone! Psalm 8 does indeed invite us to look up to the stars in wonder, but it goes on to remind us of our responsibility to the animals.

As then we study the complexity of the patterns which make up creation, perhaps trying to understand what physicists such as Stephen Hawkings have to say, it is only natural that we try to see what relevance they have to our lives, and what relevance our lives have in all these inter-locking patterns. To reduce religion to the status of a post-death insurance policy is to be as far off the mark as any horoscope seeker!

"THIS MEANS YOU"

We have to ask, therefore, at what point some part of the creation speaks to us saying "THIS MEANS YOU". We referred earlier to Martin Buber; he pointed out that there are two extremes: one is that everything in the universe seems to address me personally... then I become manic. The other is that nothing in the universe addresses me... then I become depressed.

As examples of the first extreme I think of the man who came for help because all the bus numbers added up to 666, and he felt that this meant that he was the devil. Or there was the lady who was sure that everything was telling her that she was the Virgin Mary... she can look back on that time and laugh at herself now, but at the time these two people were interpreting the details of life as if everything was speaking to them. On the other hand examples of people who feel that life is utterly meaningless are too common to need to quote in detail!

To balance these two extremes, let us remember Archbishop Temple's famous observation that he had noticed that when he prayed, coincidences seemed to happen, but when he stopped praying they seemed to stop happening!

The vital question therefore, is HOW one reads the universe... stars, coincidences and much else.

THE CLOSED BOOK

A vivid picture of how to read it is given in Revelation 5... a vision in which the book which holds the meaning of all things is laid before us, but the Book of Life remains "a closed book" even to those higher intelligences we call angels. Then the Lamb opens it... the Lamb who was slaughtered and who was raised up to life. Here is the Clue to the clue! Self-sacrificing, suffering love is the Key. Intelligence will come in once the clue is given, to follow up.

Those in whom the same Spirit of self-sacrificing love lives will be able to read the pattern of life in ever more wonderful ways. They alone can see the true meaning in the stars or anywhere else. Others will project their own patterns into what they see, and will never read the Book aright, however clever they may be.

"The skies may proclaim the glory of God" (Psalm 19) and maybe they do in ways that are more profound than we have been used to thinking, but what people see in the skies depends on what their OWN spiritual state is. "Heaven and earth are full of your glory" (Isaiah 6), but this is far from evident to the self-centred and the arrogant.

If "the Spirit of him who raised Jesus from the dead lives also in us" then we may find that the stars confirm his Word, and we shall not be surprised. But the stars must never be our primary source of guidance about the past, the present or the future. For instance, as we have already noted, many from different points of view have discerned that we are entering a new age, and the astrologers confirm this. But we are not entering the new age because the stars say so... the stars may say so because "the Lord is doing a new thing", and "the heavens declare his glory". We must get our priorities right.

THE LIVING WORD

Whatever brand of Christian we may be, we believe in a living Word which is continually speaking to us through the whole of creation, and there is nothing in the whole of creation which may not be at some time the vehicle of this Word. However we must never try to dictate to the Word the means through which he will address us. The Word of guidance, understanding or warning may come to us through the most surprising means, as in the case of the Magi who came to the child Jesus.

We must not, however, become dependent on any one channel, and above all we must beware of becoming dependent on any astrologer. Even if we accept a form of astrology, we must be aware that people tend to rely too much on "my astrologer", unable to make any decision without consulting him/her. This is the abdication of one's responsibility, and is dangerous. Such misguided people do indeed need deliverance from their bondage, to be set free to be responsible before God for their own lives.

THE FUTURE

We have noted already that popular astrology is very much concerned with the future. We have therefore to ask about the right attitude to facing the future. Sensitive human souls cannot bear the thought of a trackless desert ahead in which anything could happen. They cry out for some assurance that the future is meaningful. Astrology does seem to offer some sort of guidance here. Yet it does not say anything about the true goal of life, nor about moral values in themselves.

For instance, if "the stars say" that Tuesday is a good day for you to prosper in your financial dealings, this would apply equally to the "con man" and to the collector for Christian Aid, and it begs the question as to whether making more money would necessarily be good for you, for after all Jesus warned us that you cannot love God AND money! And as for predictions about your love-life... well!

Astrology, then, often appears to offer guidance on how YOU can negotiate your way through what lies ahead, but the assumption is that you are going your own way. What humanity needs at this crucial stage in history is a new way, a revision of our ideas about the goal of human life, and above all an awareness of the Holy Love which lies behind all things.

This is what lies behind the words of Jesus at the Last Supper: I AM THE WAY. This was said in the situation in which Thomas wanted some definite guidance on the future, which was pretty bleak at that moment! Jesus gave them the picture of middle-east travel: he was going on ahead of them, one stage at a time to prepare the way, and he would come back to guide them on the next stage of the journey. That is how caravans travelled in those days. Such a picture (often concealed by the language of our Bibles) speaks of a future which is progressive, and meaningful... it is "the journey home" and those of us who have had to travel far, know how different we feel when we realize that at last we are heading howeward! **The guidance which we are offered is in a personal relationship with him who set the stars in their courses.**

Perhaps the stars do give us some pointers, but compared with knowing him who is THE WAY, they are comparatively unimportant. If they have become a substitute for the Way, they are certainly misleading. Perhaps they were indeed God's way of leading people such as the Magi, and many others for whom the Gospel was not available, but, as the great Islamic poet Kubir said: "Behold but One in all things, it is the second which leads you astray", or as we say, "The second best is always the enemy of the best".

THE SEEKERS

When, therefore, we meet those who have turned to astrology to find some meaning in life we are very often dealing with people who have been put off belief in God by some of the things they have been told, while at the same time they still have this deep, yearning need to know what it is which is speaking to them through the created world, and to know what guidance is available. Astrology is often the first step in a person's rejection of the picture of a dead, impersonal universe with which they *thought* science confronted them. This deep need to find meaning in the universe should open a gate for us to lead them to know God.

THE MAGI

We began our examination of astrology by referring to the *magi* mentioned at the beginning of St Matthew's Gospel. Perhaps it would be a good thing to turn aside for a moment to look at the incident in detail, asking what its deeper meaning is. It makes a lovely Christmas card, and looks wonderful in the school nativity play, but... ?

The word *magi* refers to priests of the religion of Zarathushtra (Zoroaster), and they presumably lived in the east... in what is today Iran. In the year we call BC 7 there were three occasions when the planets Jupiter and Saturn came together to make a very bright "star" in "the house of Pisces". This would indicate to an astrologer that a very important king was born for the Jews. They had seen this natal star when they were in the east, they said.

Therefore they set off for the place where they would expect such a child to be born - the palace of King Herod. There is no word of a star guiding them at that point, just common sense. It is after they have been to the palace that the star is recorded as having guided them.

Now King Herod died in March BC 4, dangerously paranoid, so Jesus must have been born before BC 4. Actually it was centuries later, when they asked a monk to work out how to reckon the years from Jesus' birth, that a very simple error was made, an error which lands us with Jesus being born "before Christ" (BC)!

Presumably the thousand-mile journey would have taken about a year, and Matthew mentions that they came into the HOUSE, not the stable, and refers to Jesus as a CHILD not a baby. Hence Herod's paranoid command to kill boys under the age of two, which by our way of counting would be one. (It was later that the Arabs invented the number 0, but until then you were one when you were born.) This act fits the historical picture of Herod's old age, but the massacre of perhaps a couple of dozen children in an unimportant village is not mentioned by historians.

The strange thing is that it is St Matthew who records this. He is the most traditionally Jewish of all the Gospel writers, so it all the more surprising that it is he who brings in men from another religion, guided by astrology which the Bible of his day condemned! It must have gone against the grain for him to write it down.

Surely the message is that Jesus came to fulfil what was good in other religions, not to tell them they were wrong. However tradition has built up a picture of three kings coming to the manger along with the shepherds, and has lost the point about relating to other religions. A very negative attitude to other religions has done so much harm!

God is not bound by our dogmas, however sure we may be that they are right. Perhaps words from a poem by Ian Fraser are worth quoting here:

Our God contrives
footholds where none are seen; and meets
hesitant steps of faith with ground
conjured out of nothing. So our way
is sure, only when robbed of evidence.
I walk this day
like one who walked on waves.

CONCLUSIONS

* **It is through our prayer and Bible study, through the Word and the Sacraments that we are to know THE WAY, and to steer our course through life, with due regard to such environmental factors as affect us, possibly including the stars.**

* **We must beware of allowing any astrologer or astrological system to form a bondage over us. In the Power of God's Spirit we are meant to have dominion over the elemental forces, such as astral influences, not to be subject to them. (Colossians 2:20 NEB)**

THE WHISPERER

The next forbidden activity is *nachash*. Now the usual meaning of this word is THE SERPENT, but it also links up with WHISPERING or HISSING.

We find that it comes into the Bible in two places, giving us an idea of the meaning here. The first is in Genesis 30:27. Jacob says to Laban, his uncle and employer, that he has learned through *nachash* that the Lord had blessed Laban because of Jacob's presence. Now it may mean that there was a whispered rumour through the camp, but it is more likely to mean that he had received it as guidance from God through some means or other.

Not long after that, in Genesis 44:5,15 it occurs again, when Joseph's servants find the cup which has been "planted" in the brothers' baggage, and they are accused of theft. The servant explains that it is the cup which Joseph uses for *nachash*.

From this we note three things:

(1) Jacob and Joseph both use *nachash* without any sign of disapproval, even though it is one of the forbidden activities in Deuteronomy 18:10.

58

(2) It would seem to involve whispering, and an object such as a cup. Presumably Joseph would look into the cup and begin to whisper, getting information this way. It looks like a primitive form of reading tea-cups combined with a form of "tongues" resulting in "a word of knowledge".

(3) This does not seem to be decision-making, as it was with the first two things we looked at, but rather a way of getting information from a supernatural source. The Canaanite prophet Balaam was hired by King Balak to practise divination against the threat of Israel - the context of Numbers 24:1 indicates, however, that *nachash* simply provided information.

Of course in the Bible as always people often seek augury such as this to be one up on competitors or enemies. It is this use which is condemned, and many stories of the ancients tell how augury was a double edged weapon, turning out to mean something less favourable than had been thought at first.

Using such means to be 'one up' on your competitors or enemies is not a right use of supernatural powers. It was precisely this which Jesus refused to do when he was aware that he could have called on twelve legions of angels, but did not.

We have a very important principle here, then: **God, and the whole supernatural realm, is not there to be called on to further *our* plans, or to be called in and manoeuvered to suit us.**

DEPENDENCY

The danger in all these things is that they are addictive. Once a person does get an accurate word of knowledge or good guidance on what decision to make, it is only too easy to become dependent on the person who provided it. We may joke about reading tea-cups, but people *do* become addicted to it, and find themselves in bondage of a sort, unable to make decisions responsibly. We saw the same problem with astrology.

Having said that we must in fairness note that the same can happen in a Charismatic group, when they become dependent on the person with the gift of prophecy, or knowledge or healing. What began as a true acceptance of God's guidance, becomes an unhealthy dependency, and the whole group disintegrates. There is a very fine line between obedience and dependency.

7 WITCHES AND DOCTORS

THE WITCH

There seems to be agreement in all versions that the next word *kashaf* refers to being a sorcerer, or witch. The Hebrew word literally means A CUTTER. If you remember that scene in *Macbeth* when the witches on the blasted heath are chopping things up to make their potion, you will see the connection between chopping up and witchcraft!

When the Hebrew Bible was translated into Greek for Jews who could no longer speak Hebrew (about a century before Jesus), they translated this as *pharmax*. In the Book of Revelation one of the categories of people who are not to be found in the Holy City is the *pharmax* (Rev 21:8). That seems pretty hard on your local chemist (pharmacist)!

Lest we feel that our local pharmacy is a branch of hell, look at what has actually happened. The pharmax of Biblical days, and indeed right up to Shakespeare's time, was somebody who brewed up spells, poisons, potions, medicines etc. A potion to make somebody fall in love with you, a poison or a curse to liquidate your enemy, a herbal remedy for an illness were all part of the stock in trade of the witch, the *pharmax*. Gradually these functions came to be separated. The monasteries developed medicinal drugs and herbs, indeed as I write I am aware that not far away, on Soutra Hill, a mediaeval monastic hospital is being excavated, in whose ruins they are finding opium and various other medicinal drugs and herbs. That shows us that one part of the *pharmax*'s trade was being hived off to the church.

We spoke earlier of CLUSTERS, and in this case we see that over the last two centuries the cluster of the *pharmax* is being undone, and the elements separated out. Yet this is a recent thing, from the point of view of human history. Even in the 17th century in Perth an old lady was burned as a witch because she had healed a cow in the Name of the Holy Trinity. She was counted in the same category as the Morayshire witches, at whose trial it became evident that they did indeed indulge in a lot of very harmful practices, and really believed that they had the devil at their gatherings. The idea that they were innocent, deluded, harmless old women is very far off the mark. Of course in many cases they *were* innocent or deluded, and also many of the witch-hunters were themselves obsessed and even "tarred with the same brush" as the real witches, yet there was a real issue at stake.

However the medicinal side has gradually shaken itself free of the other elements, so that the modern pharmacist, while descended from the pharmax, is no longer part of the cluster which was condemned. This brings us back to another point we have looked at: that some activities are not evil in themselves, although part of a cluster which is

So now we must move on to sort out the various strands:

* Medicine - regular and homoeopathic
* Herbalism
* Witchcraft today

THE MEDICAL PROFESSION

The Old Testament has very little about medicine and healing, and in this it is unlike the religions of the neighbouring nations. We know for instance that the priests of Egypt were skilful in the healing arts, and the Greeks had their healing temples. The Old Testament however has very little about healing as such, and while archeology has discovered Jewish skeletons with signs of wounds having been treated, there is no evidence of "medicine" such as is found from the graves of surrounding nations.

The Old Testament seemed to see illness as God's punishment for sin. Therefore the right thing to do was to repent, and to keep at it until God forgave you... healing being the sign that you were forgiven. Psalm after psalm continues this theme of equating healing with forgiveness*. Of course if you believe this, then seeking to be healed medically is trying to get round God's judgment. Going to a *pharmax* for medicine instead of repenting would never do! This view, of course, is challenged in the Book of Job, and even in some other psalms.

* Compare, for instance Psalm 103 in which healing and forgiveness are equated, with Psalm 73 in which the psalmist complains at how unfair life seems sometimes.

When Jesus came he took a different line. In Mark 2 when he heals the boy let down through the roof, he deliberately challenges the pharisees in their attitude to illness, and throughout his ministry he healed without the moralising which people expected.

The Church has not always followed her Master's line on this, often reverting to the Old Testament view. For instance in the Counter Reformation in France there was at one point a law that it was illegal to call in the doctor before you had called in the priest, assuming that confession of the sin was the real basis of healing. The prayers for the sick in the Reformed Chuches were much on the same line, assuming that submitting to God's judgment, and seeking his pardon were the primary concerns in healing, with medicine coming as a back-up.

It is, of course, obvious that wrong living does lead to illness, and equally that right living will encourage health, yet the link is not quite as obvious as to say: "If you have a bad illness, then you must have done something to deserve it!" Let us think, for instance, of the thousands of children who will develop cancer as the result of the Chernobyl disaster. Would anybody be rash enough to say that they, or their families are worse than those who survived unscathed? Jesus dealt with this in cases such as that of the man born blind (John 9:3), when he specifically denied a sin-link, but simply saw the occasion as a way of revealing the glory of God.   In our own time we see medicine as just that... a way of revealing the glory of God, and the history of medical missions works this out in detail. The National Health Service in our country is the outcome of much Christian influence. We see God's love in the care and skill of doctors and nurses... and in our local *pharmax*! We may indeed query some aspects of medicine and the drug industry, but not on the grounds that they are witchcraft!

HOMOEOPATHY

This is the next strand we sort out from the old *pharmax*. New Age people seem to tend towards HOMEOPATHY, whereas Charismatic literature is quite sure that it is of the devil.

Some Christian doctors and nurses feel that homoeopathic treatment shows more respect for the sanctity of human life than much modern medicine. On the other hand in *Healing at any Price?*, Samuel Pfeifer cites cases where following homeopathic treatment, psychic disturbances have emerged and there has been a loss of faith in Jesus. He and other Charismatic writers also give examples of doctors who, on deeper spiritual experience, have renounced their homoeopathy.

We clearly have to take both sides seriously. First let us ask what homoeopathy is. Drs David Taylor Reilly & Morag Taylor in *Complementary Medical Research* (Routledge) say this:

> Homoeopathy asks us to reconsider the basic way we view symptoms and their treatment.   Successful conventional drug therapy tends to follow two paths: either it aims to block

unwanted reactions, or it substitutes for the body's own response... Homoeopathy pursues a third therapeutic avenue - it attempts to stimulate auto-regulatory responses.

In other words it is:

The treatment of like with like, to find a match between the disease syndrome of an individual patient and the syndrome provoked by a drug in healthy subjects... (*What is Homoeopathy?* by Dr Peter Fisher)

The best known version of this approach is our smallpox vaccination. So far so good, nobody could fault that. The problems begin to arise when we look at how the remedies are made. The process is called "potentization". Dr Fisher writes:

The medicine is repeatedly diluted 1:100 and shaken hard after each dilution. One dilution gives a 1 in 100 dilution; two 1 in 10,000; after three dilutions, the starting material has been diluted 1 in a million, and so on. It can be calculated from the scientific principle known as as Avogadro's Law, that if this process is repeated 12 times or more, the resulting dilution is very unlikely to contain a single molecule of the starting substance. This means that, whatever it is that causes homoeopathic medicines to have their effect, it is not the substance. It is thought that the effects are mediated by the microstructure of water.

Pfeifer in *Healing at Any Price?* and Roy Livesey in *Beware Alternative Medicine* clearly think that something occult, magical occurs in this process. There is the suggestion that in the process of shaking some occult force is passed from the healer through the water. Yet this is clearly not the case when the preparation is done by ordinary workers in a laboratory using a vibrator... the usual thing these days.

The conventional medical view is that these remedies are just *placebos* - any real effects should not be attributed to the medicine, but to the personal care and to the power of "suggestion". Yet in the above paper by Drs Taylor Reilly and Taylor, proper research projects are referred to, and in *Research in Homoeopathy* Dr Fisher refers to the fact that homoeopathy has been used down on the farm by vets such as Christopher Day, and has been found useful. Animals do not respond to *placebos*!

However, the type of doctor who is adventurous enough to try out homoeopathy, may be adventurous in other directions too! So we often find such doctors dabbling in other areas which we have touched on in this book. We are up against the issue which we looked at in "Clusters". Homoeopathy is often only part of a cluster which may involve all sorts of things. This would make us cautious.

Perhaps, if one is consulting homoeopaths, one should be clear as to whether they are ordinary doctors who use such remedies when required, or whether they have opened themselves to forces on the psychic level which they are not necessarily spiritually capable of handling. We will also be on our guard if they are propagating "spiritual" views which are out of harmony with what we believe.

Another aspect to take into account is that by its very nature homoeopathy tends to treat the whole person, reacting against so much in modern medicine which focuses on the diseased part only. This in itself is good, but as we have seen throughout this book, the higher up the spectrum, the more crucial are the issues. For instance, if I had broken my leg, my main concern would be that it should be set by somebody who was a good orthopaedic surgeon, whatever his personal life was like! But if I suffered from some psycho-somatic disease, I would be very careful whom I allowed to start exploring my inner life. We therefore have to be on our guard when it comes to "treating the whole person".

CONCLUSIONS

The basic teaching of treating like with like cannot be faulted, in fact many people see it as more consistent with their Christian Faith than allopathic (ordinary) medicine.

The whole system of potentization sets us a lot of problems, but if the remedies can be made up by any pharmacist, and can be shown to be effective, then they are no different from other remedies.

The emphasis on treating the whole person, and not just the disease, is good and in line with Christian understanding. Yet we have to be on our guard against wrong influences in a way that is not so necessary in allopathic medicine. We have to be conscious that when going to a homoeopathic practitioner, it is quite possible that the homoeopathy is part of a cluster which may include elements which we would reject.

A lot more theological and scientific research is needed!

HERBAL MEDICINE

Now we look at another strand in what was the witch's stock-in-trade: HERBALISM. Herbs have an ancient place in the life of

Christian people, for instance, St Columba himself prescribed herbs, and there is the story of the leper woman in Harris who, banished to the sea-shore, cured herself with herbs and sang:

> There no plant in all the land
> but blooms replete with Thy Virtue.
> Each form in all the sweeping strand,
> with joy replete Thou dost endue;
> Jesus, Jesus, Jesus,
> unto whom all praise is due!
>
> (*The Cry of the Deer*, David Adam, p.51)

When we read such a story we therefore wonder why people such as Pfeifer and Livesey warn us against herbalism as something evil. Yet they do and we must try to understand, and to look at these cures, which are often rooted in folk-lore. There is nothing in the Bible directly against medicines and herbs, although more often it mentions anointing with oil which was part of normal medical treatment. There is, however, in the book of Sirach in the Apocrypha, the observation that "God makes the earth yield healing herbs which the prudent man should not neglect".

In our day many of the old nature cures are coming back, partly because so many modern drugs are dangerous and have side-effects, so that people are looking for gentler healing methods. However a recent report has warned people that herbal cures *can* have side-effects too, and that there is much "quackery" in this field! It makes the point too that a semi-skilled person, who perhaps knows much about herbs, is not always in a position to make a correct diagnosis, and is therefore even more likely to make mistakes than the fully trained medical doctor! However that practical concern is not what Pfeifer and Livesey are warning us against.

MYTHS

Let us look for a possible reason, then. When we look back at the folk-lore, we see that often the reasons why certain flowers were thought to be connected with certain illnesses or with certain parts of the body were ridiculous by our standards. However, in every country people create myths to explain things, so that when a plant was found to have a beneficial effect, people would develop a myth to explain it. This, of course does not deny that at the same time many genuine discoveries were made, and modern medicine has to come back to them at times. The objection to herbalism seems then to be rooted in the association of herbs with pagan "gods" and myths. We explain the effects by our own myth: "science"!

CLUSTERS

On the other hand, it may well be on the principle of clusters... some herbal remedies are good, and perhaps preferable to some medical drugs whose long-term effects are unknown; but they can also be part of a cluster of all sorts of things. The person who prescribes them may be just a person who has this skill and knowledge, or we may find that this is the thin end of a very large wedge.

ASTROLOGY

Perhaps the biggest objection to herbalism is that very often herbalists assert that plants should be planted and harvested at certain points in the astrological cycle. Ronald Black of the School of Scottish Studies wrote a very interesting article on *The Glorious Lamp of the Poor* in which he remembers how even recently it was taken for granted in the Highlands that there was a right and a wrong moon-time for planting, harvesting and slaughtering animals. This of course reminds people of the old witchcraft and sets them on guard. Perhaps, however, it can be shown that there is an objective difference involved, one that is available for universal use; if it is objective fact then it is part of God's good creation, and it can be used for good. It is a matter for experiment, and I have been told that such experiments are being made in Germany and Switzerland by Maria Thun.

A THEORY

In the light of this, I would like to propose a theory, which people can study and discuss:

The nature-forces referred to above affecting the growth of plants are in their rightful place when we consider plants, and we are right to take them into account. Where it is wrong to do so, is allowing them to affect us when we are making decisions which should be made on moral/spiritual grounds. By allowing them into areas which are inappropriate, we upset the balance of nature and that is where the whole thing becomes demonic.

I know that this is very debatable, but I put it here in order to get it debated... prayerfully and logically. See also chapter 11.

HOOKED

The final objection to herbalism is that people tend to get hooked on nature-cures, though this is just another version of the hypochondria well-known to the medical profession. (My personal observation, not backed up by statistics, would suggest that the rate among those who go for nature cures is higher than among patients of ordinary doctors). One finds very unhealthy people with their cupboards stacked with nature cures, and always going for more. It is possible that actual "bondages" form, which need to be broken, especially if the person selling or prescribing the "cures" has a cluster which includes unhealthy elements.

But why do people get hooked? Here as elsewehere it is because they are looking for an answer in the wrong place. The nature cure may be *part* of the answer, but the real answer lies in the depths where the person must face God, others and himself/herself. However, that is not to condemn nature cures in themselves, any more than we condemn all medicines because some people are hypochondriac. We have an important principle here:

Because something is abused, it is not necessarily evil in itself.

CONCLUSION

* **There are many healing herbs, and a knowledge of them is one way of serving God and humanity.**

* **Individal herbalists work on different bases. In some cases they may seek to draw you into practices which go far beyond herbalism, into a dangerous cluster.**

* **We have to accept the practical limitations, especially in diagnosis.**

* **We must beware of becoming hooked.**

8 "HEALING"

The aspects of the work of the pharmax at which we have looked so far have all been medical in some form, but now we come to the non-medical side, and the problem is what to call it! The whole subject and its terminology is a minefield.

PSYCHIC AND SPIRITUAL

If the heading were "Faith Healing" then most people would know what was meant, but this is a very misleading term. It emphasizes a degree of credulity, or gullibility. It has overtones of the use of "suggestion" and mild hypnosis. Yet this is *not* what FAITH means. If we look at Hebrews 11 we see that faith is that quality which leads people to step out into the unknown, or to face impossible odds on the basis of a strong inner conviction of truth and rightness. It is the very opposite of being suggestible and credulous!

For another thing, while faith does play a part, more important is the fact that somebody has learned how to tap into a power-source which is not usually known to be available. In the case of ministering to somebody unconscious, or to a baby, it is obviously not "faith" in the patient which "does the trick"; it is the power operating through those ministering.

HEALING AND "LEVELS OF CREATION"

Let us begin by being clear that God has built healing into every level of the creation. There is a sort of self-righting principle in the universe as well as an "auto-destruct" principle of which death is the main example. It is this self-righting principle which the Bible refers to as God's RIGHTEOUSNESS, although the modern use of this word makes it unusable! I remember the Professor of Hebrew leaning over his desk at us and saying, "If a Hebrew's car were going smoothly, he would say it was a righteous car." Perhaps RIGHTNESS is a better word.

If "healing", then, is aligning ourselves with the rightness of God, built into life at every level, we should be clear about the various levels. Let us look at them:

At the physical level there are chemicals which have a healing effect. There are plants with healing potential, as we have seen. There are many healing things we can do at this level: from making a cup of tea to performing an operation.

At the psychic level there is much that flows between people bringing healing. I remember a doctor telling me that he had read a report from a drug company which noticed that Doctor A always seemed to have more positive results to report from new medicines than Doctor B. This was so widespread that they had concluded that some doctors were themselves the factor which made the difference. The 'A' doctors radiated something at the psychic level without realising it. Most of us have probably had experience of people who seemed to have this gift.

At the intellectual level we find answers to illness. We use our brains to work out, for instance why the baby is crying more than usual, or why there are more cases of cancer in certain districts than in others.

At the spiritual level, when somebody enters into deep communion with God, lifting some sufferer with him/her, then the all-creative love of God flows in deep healing.

At the first levels, mineral, vegetable, physical, psychic, intellectual, we may or may not see God. The leper woman in Harris saw Jesus in the plants which had healed her, but many people operate successfully without direct reference to God. At the truly spiritual level, however, it is "God or nothing!"

One comes across many who sincerely work for the good of other people at some level, and while they are not perfect, they have a feel of "rightness" about them, even though they do not claim to be God-inspired, Christian or religous. To condemn them as evil is ridiculous, and often counter-productive. On the other hand there are those who make much of being Christian, claiming to work on the spiritual level, but who have a very un-right feel about them!

HEALTH WARNING!

This whole area of healing is indeed a minefield strewn with subtle traps laid for the unwary: take the example of the person with basic psychic healing gifts. After having cured somebody, this person says modestly, "It was God not me." That sounds like modesty, anyway! Yet what is really being said? First of all it is a claim that the healer is in a special relationship with God, because it would seem that God has responded to him/her in a way He does not seem to respond to others. Secondly it is a claim to humility. Thirdly, nobody is left in any doubt that this person is "a healer". What comes across is a smug arrogance!

The fact is that a natural healing gift is "of God" in the same way that a gift for playing music or mathematical skill is a gift of God. No more, no less. It does not imply that the person is necessarily "in tune" with God. In fact the religious, or even Christian jargon may hide real danger.

PSYCHIC HEALING

The basic idea is that there are energies which can be channelled into healing... or into curses, hexes and so on, as the old *pharmaxes* knew well! Most of humanity prior to modern "scientific" man has understood something of these energies. They are discerned by very sensitive people through meditation, but have not been discovered by "scientific" means. Dowsing is often used to trace them. Such is the underlying assumption.

New Age people see a universe in which there are complex patterns of energy. At earth's surface they speak of ley lines, within the human beings they speak of the *chakras* and lines upon which acupuncture depends, and beyond us in the universe are the energies referred to in astrology.

These energies, if they exist, are not personal, and so are not themselves psychic, even though it is through the psychic aspect of humanity that they are known. (In some cases discarnate spirits are invoked, but we deal with that later.) The human spirit with its will-power can rise above their influence and can actually influence them. Incidentally, it is worth noting that those who *do* discern these things are very disturbed at what humanity is doing at this level, and issue strong warnings; for instance they say that many of our current human activities disrupt the ley line patterns of energy and this causes serious disorder in the long run.

There are many books these days, mostly from the USA, about how to channel these energies for healing. Some of these books refer to God in the background, and some have no reference to God at all. They are mostly marketed for people asking, "How can *I* be a healer?"... a dangerous ego-trip.

OBJECTIONS

This is where the Charismatic books smell a demonic rat. So let us try to track it down. *First*, they rightly see the danger of self-centered ego-tripping. *Second*, the critics assert that there is nothing in the Bible about these energies, so that either they do not exist or else, if they do, they must be satanic. But this is ridiculous, for there is nothing in the Bible about radio waves, atomic energy, X-rays or many other things which are now part of our lives. The Bible points us to the nature of God, as revealed in the life of Jesus. Exploring earth and its hidden riches is the business of the human race.

Just as human intelligence has discovered electricity and atomic energy, so perhaps it is re-discovering these earth-energies. As we know well, the way in which we are using atomic power, oil and many other energy sources is threatening the future of the planet. Each time we make a new discovery for the good of mankind, the Old Enemy manages to twist it to destructive uses. No doubt the same applies here. Perhaps we would do well not to be too naive!

A *third* objection is that these energies were observed by non-Christian religions. Now, while they are not actually part of the teachings of the Buddha or of the main Hindu philosophers, they are common knowledge in the east, and in many other places. It is often, however in their Indian and Chinese forms that we receive them. Charismatic writers go on to allege that knowledge of them is part of a satanic plot to undermine Christianity, and to replace it with a vague oriental form of religion.

Yet learning about these energies is not itself "religion". Religion *determines the use* one makes of energies which one has discovered... be it oil or psychic energy.

Whether or not there are these wonderful, interlinking patterns of energy, all mathematically balanced, as Gordon Strachan makes out, is the real issue. Just because it was people in a more intuitive society who became aware of these energies, it does not mean to say that they are wrong. This takes us back to the point we made when looking at Homoeopathy: because a discovery about the nature of the world is made by an atheistic scientist, or by somebody of another religion, it does not mean to say that it is wrong. Because the discovery is adopted into the world-view of the atheist or of the Buddhist, it does not prevent us from asking where it fits into the world-view in which we believe.

CURING AND HEALING

One final objection to various forms of "healing" is that it seems to enable people to evade the challenge of the Gospel in that it appears to offer peace of mind through, for instance, some form of massage, or through some herbal treatment.

Yet one could say the same of regular medicine, in that people

71

can seek health and peace of mind for themselves and for others from pills instead of seeking it from God. Nevertheless it is considered right for the doctor to prescribe a pain-killer or a sedative at times, without losing sight of the fact that the answer eventually must lie in a new relationship with God.

At all levels of healing people *begin* by wanting somebody with some special knowledge to take away their symptoms. It is right that we should respond by seeking to do so with whatever skills or powers we have. Yet at all levels "curing" only becomes "making whole" when the person sees far beyond this and becomes an active agent in his/her own healing, so that the whole experience becomes a learning experience... learning about self and about God.

THE CONTRASTS

The psychic level and the spiritual level are easily confused. Look at some contrasts:

In PSYCHIC healing there are techniques to be learned, and facts to be taken into account. In SPIRITUAL healing we are concerned with a personal relationship with God in Christ, and with the patient. There are no techniques, and the only question is the depth of communion.

At the PSYCHIC level we can all develop our potential to channel healing, some more easily than others. We can gain more knowledge about the vital energies in the human make-up and in the universe. At the SPIRITUAL level there is only the breaking down in successive stages of the outer "self" in order to be more open to God and to people.

The person with a NATURAL gift will be led to lay hands on the afflicted part in a certain way, and to keep them there until the power switches off. The person working on the SPIRITUAL level may or may not be led to lay hands on the afflicted part. Often it is rather to take the other's hand or to lay hands on the head in blessing.

Each person working at the PSYCHIC level tends to be more successful with certain types of trouble. At the SPIRITUAL level the type of trouble is quite irrelevant.

At the PSYCHIC level certain people are more gifted than others. At the SPIRITUAL level healings are the by-product of the prayer of the Christian fellowship. When the "two or three are gathered in the Name of Jesus" to focus the Love of God on a sufferer then, even if none of them has a natural gift, the Holy Spirit can bestow a gift of healing to meet the occasion. (Hence the strange wording in the Greek of 1 Corinthians 12: "GiftS of healingS"... not "THE gift of healing" as in some modern translations.) This Gift of the Spirit is usually discovered when in natural compassion, people reach out to express the love of God by touch, and find that something more than sympathy has flowed.

At the PSYCHIC level it is very important that when healing, one's body should be in a healthy, fit state, with the energy flowing smoothly. At the SPIRITUAL level, God often uses us when we are at the end of our tether, with nothing to give physically.

These, then, are some of the contrasts between the two levels. The ideal is when a person with a natural gift finds his/her place in the Christian Fellowship, so that the totality of God's creation can operate. In the life of the group, people should feel that "in this case it should be so-and-so who lays on hands."

TWO-LEVEL MINISTRY

Many if not all of the "big names" in healing have this two-level psychic/spiritual ministry, and they have a special need to be kept within the discipline of prayer and Bible study, for it is only too easy to slip down on to the psychic level, and then there is trouble, disruption and all sorts of ills.

To explain this further: many of these ministers, priests and others who are well-known for their healing gifts would hotly deny that what they have is a natural healing gift, enhanced by the Gifts of the Spirit. They would claim that it is *all* of the the Spirit. This becomes a danger for them, because if healings go on happening, then they perhaps do not notice that they are slipping spiritually. What had begun as God's calling so easily turns into *my* profession without our realising it! Some of them become very egotistical and domineering. All sorts of troubles ensue. This is why they need the framework of Christian fellowship and discipline if they are to remain healthy.

It seems that this is what had happened to the church in Corinth, in which obviously from what St Paul said, there were plenty of healings, tongues and other Gifts of the Spirit, but at the same time there was division and all sorts of wrong-living, which he deals with one at a time. They had become so obsessed with the work of the Holy Spirit at the psychic level, that they had slipped from a true spirituality. We have seen the same thing happen today in charismatic groups.

73

HEALING AND THE CHURCH

Healing should be a straight continuation of the work of Jesus. However the grim fact is that even though the early church carried on healing in the Name of Jesus for several centuries, it eventually dropped out; and anybody with a healing gift was then liable to become a victim of one of the periodic witch-hunts. So-called "saints" who were safely dead could be accredited with healing miracles in the Roman Catholic Church, but it was a risky thing to do if you were still living!

Then, at the beginning of the 20th century, healing began to be restored to its rightful place in the life of the church under the influence of a movement in the Anglican Church, led by James Moore Hickson, a layman. Later, when the Renewal movement came along, healing was seen as a Gift of the Spirit, and once more in some places the church is seen as an agent of healing in the Name of Jesus. However we have a long way to go before it has its rightful place.

TO BE A HEALER?

If a person does have a *psychic* gift of healing, it is his/her responsibility to train it and to learn as much about technique as possible. This is because psychic energies, like electricity and atomic energy are part of the creation, and therefore subject to laws which must be observed if they are to be used for healing... or for anything else. For instance if people are healing by laying hands at this level, it is important to get the position of the hands exactly right, and to wash hands after ministering. People who dabble without being properly grounded in a knowledge of the basic laws may do harm to the patients and to themselves. Above all they must remember that to seek psychic development beyond the point at which their *spiritual* development can control it, is dangerous, for the person and for others. It is important to face the moral and spiritual choices which go along with this knowledge.

To say, as some do, that any *natural* healing gift is satanic indicates a warped view of God's Creation. Rather the natural healer - AND THE DOCTOR AND THE NURSE - should be encouraged in and by the Church. They are all subject to intense pressure. They are all at times crushed by situations in which they feel helpless. They are all tempted to ego-trip. They all need help.

HOW SHOULD WE REACT TO A NATURAL HEALER?

When people came to the Christian Fellowship of Healing claiming to be healers, we took a positive line: "Join in our Bible study and prayer life. Then, if we all feel that it is right, we may call on you to help." If they went away disgusted, we had been spared problems. If they joined in so that their natural gift was caught up in the Body of Christ by the Holy Spirit, we had gained valuable fellow-workers. Perhaps this may be a guide.

One cannot say, then, that if a person discovers a healing gift, it is wrong to develop it, even if developing it does lead into psychic and spiritual dangers. As we have seen, since developing on the psychic level is "higher up the scale", it is more liable to negative influences in the psychic environment than with a doctor exploring medical things.

MOTIVES

If we feel drawn to exercise some aspect of the ministry of healing, we have to be rigorous with ourselves about our motives. "Are my motives really pure, free from pride, greed, ego-centricity, fascination with the supernatural, need for admiration and approval? Am I motivated purely by compassion?"

If my answer is: "YES, I am free from all such sinful faults" then I should not touch healing at all! Such self-righteousness and self-deception is dangerous. Only those who know their own weaknesses, and who are in a fellowship in which those weaknesses are known can be trusted with healing: "If we say we have no sin we deceive ourselves", as St John pointed out, and self-deception is lethal.

If we are seeking healing and find ourselves confronted with somebody who seems to be working at the psychic level, be they Christian or not, then we must be on our guard. On the other hand Christians have no right to assume, as many do, that anybody with a natural healing gift is psychically unclean. We need rather to examine ourselves for spiritual pride, jealousy and paranoia.

If a congregation or fellowship feels drawn to a greater emphasis on healing, that is good. They should be careful to concentrate on the purely spiritual level on the one hand, and on the practical, down-to-earth response to suffering humanity on the the other. Then such Gifts of the Spirit as they need will be given them when they need them. They will be taught what they need to know as they become ready for new teaching.

LOOKING BACK ON THE *PHARMAX*

We have looked at the medical and para-medical descendants of the old pharmax, leaving witchcraft to be dealt with separately. While in some ways the aspects at which we have looked are very different from each other, yet there are elements which they have in common. For instance:

On the practitioner side *all* healing, at whatever level, is a happy hunting ground for cranks, for ego-trippers, for power-seekers and for those who are dishonest. Even those who begin out of real compassion can slip.

On the patient side, all healing, but especially Alternative Medicine, is especially attractive to lonely, inadequate and gullible people.

Because of this we need to be extra careful with Alternative Medicine practitioners, for while the BMA tries to safeguard the regular medical side, there is no such safeguard on the nature cure side.

INCONSISTENCY

Thinking through these things we find a strange inconsistency in many Charismatic books: Acupuncture, Homeopathy and Herbalism are condemned as diabolic on the grounds that they come from non-Christian understandings of humanity. The objectors refer, for instance, to the fact that Hahnemann who started Homoeopathy was a Freemason and had been affected by oriental thought.

Yet, as we noted earlier in this book, the same writers accept modern western medicine almost uncritically, even though it is based on a materialistic view of humanity which contradicts the Christian view, and if we withdrew all medical knowledge gained by men who were "masons", we would have little left!

On the other hand, of course, many New Age people scorn modern medicine as "reductionist", which is to say, it REDUCES the person to a collection of bits, each with a "specialist" who knows all about that bit, but who may well lose sight of the PERSON! (Only recently I met a person who came away from seeing a specialist, humiliated and angry, having been treated as a mere bit of machinery which is not working properly. Thank God not all specialists are like that, but it happens far too often.)

So here again we find the Charismatics seeing the devil in the New Age people, while the New Age people see the modern, depersonalized system as diabolic. "**It is easy to see where the devil is at work in others**".

ORIENTAL IDEAS

To take things a step further, let us take two very important ideas which come to us from the East - anathema to many Christian writers.

YIN-YANG

The Chinese idea of balancing the various apparently opposite sides of our natures is an important one, and some Christians would do well to learn something of balance! Many modern Charismatic books inveigh against the idea because it lacks a doctrine of sin. That is all very well, but even the Ten Commandments seem to be based on the idea that we *could* obey God's Law if we tried hard enough, and the prophets assume that too. St Paul knew better! Neither YIN-YANG nor the Ten Commandments, then, match up to the full Christian insight into the human condition. Both, *taken out of context* are inadequate. Yet there is something to be learned from both.

Just because some pearl of wisdom comes from another culture, and is not the complete Gospel, we should not therefore discard it or see it as demonic. We should rather look to see where it is fulfilled in Christ.

ENERGY FLOW

Another area of conflict arises because through intense introspection over centuries, Orientals claim to have discovered a pattern of energy-flow in the body. This is the basis of acupuncture and of some other healing techniques. Western medicine has not found any such thing. We are faced here with a simple question of FACT. Are there or are there not such energy patterns? If there are, and some western practitioners are experimenting in this field, then it must fit into the Gospel somehow. We do not need to swallow the rest of the cluster.

As we shall see when we look at the final chapter on the opening of St John's Gospel, fundamental Christian teaching affirms that the Light enlightens every person, and therefore has not been absent from Hindu and Chinese sages. We must sift carefully knowledge from whatever source, be it Hindu wise man, Marxist scientist, or western materialistic doctor. We may have to do quite a lot of re-thinking, but to reject it all out of hand is foolish.

SOME CONCLUSIONS

Because non-Christians perceive some truth or fact before Christians do, this does not mean that the insight is wrong.
Because Communists, Hindus or Buddhists have arrived at certain

conclusions about the way human beings work, we cannot dismiss such insights out of hand. A valid insight into the working of the universe, and the human body or into the effects of certain herbs will naturally be explained in terms of the mythology of the society in which those concerned live. We can accept the insight without being bound by the myths.

The oriental sages' methods have been deep introspection, whereas ours have been by physical observation and analysis. Both have their values, and both can be part of a cluster of non-Christian ideas, and need to be thought through.

Although over the centuries we have separated pharmacy from the rest of the *pharmax's* trade, we still need to be wary, whether our *pharmax* is our doctor, our chemist or our nature-cure practitioner. We must guard against addictions at every level of healing.

Looking back on all the modern versions of the pharmax, we have to note one thing which applies to them all:

No drugs, medicines or "cures" can be effective if the illness is rooted in wrong attitudes, e.g. the love of money, hurt pride leading to resentment, and so on. While we reject the over-simplification of "You must have done something to deserve it", we cannot escape the fact that each illness or accident is a learning experience, and that in and through this, God does have something to say to the sufferer.

It is particularly important to note, in our society, that if a person is suffering from one of the stress diseases, then soothing drugs or herbs are only a temporary answer, sooner or later the person must change his life style... or REPENT, to use the old word! (Remember that "Repent" means to re-think, not to become morbidly introspective!)

FINALLY

* **There is healing potential, a rightness, at every level of life, and humanity is meant to discover these and to use them responsibly.**

* **People with a special interest in healing should operate within a fellowship concerned with the wholeness of the Gospel, so that they can be protected from the subtle temptations which beset the "healer".**

* No individual has *the* gift of healing all disease. We all have gifts in some direction but it takes us all together to represent the healing ministry of Jesus.

* No single person has *all* the answers for any other person; we must always accept that our gift is only one part of God's answer. Being possesive about one's "patients" is fatal.

* **Where we are truly experiencing "the Fellowship of the Holy Spirit" anybody may find himself/herself involved in the healing of any condition.** "Nothing is incurable, there are only incurable people", as somebody said.

Valid discoveries may be made in places where they are taken into a religion or philosophy which is at odds with Christianity. We have to sort out the grain from the chaff.

9 TODAY'S MAGIC?

WITCHCRAFT

There was a time when we regarded witches as fun-figures for Hallowe'en, leftovers from a superstitious past, and we thought that the witch-hunts were examples of poor innocent old women being persecuted for delusions. Strangely, today we are having to change our minds. An example of this was when an intelligent, attractive young woman came to the Christian Fellowship of Healing. She wanted to leave her coven because they wanted her children (one dreads to think for what purposes). This meant a deep spiritual struggle. She had to undo many of the rituals in which she had been involved, and to be cleansed from the uncleanness of it all.

When they heard that she was coming over to Christianity the coven took action. Threatening letters came through the door, letters which were really frightening. We suggested that she tell the police. Her answer was: "The local police are in the coven... if I did report it, it would make it worse." So we found that both at the material level and at the psychic level we were in for a long, hard fight. We were not up against deluded old women!

In a way it is strange that "sorcerer" comes in the middle of those verses in Deuteronomy (18:10-11), for the practices mentioned are more or less a catalogue of the witches' stock-in-trade. Therefore, in a sense, we are dealing with the whole text when we deal with "witch". Two main themes lie behind the practice:

(1) In "black" witchcraft Satan, the devil, is called up and they enter into a relationship with it.

(2) Natural forces, as yet unkown to Western "scientific" man are harnessed either for good ("white" witches) or for evil ("black" witches).

BLACK WITCHCRAFT

Calling up the devil seems to be a bit of mediaeval nonsense, yet we had the case of the lad who came to us in a frightened state for advice. He worked on a building site, and in the lunch-hour one of the men had said that he had found in a magazine how to call up the devil... they thought they would do it to pass the time, "for a lark". The lad concerned was enough of a Christian to know that he wanted nothing to do with it and left them to it. When he came back he found a very frightened bunch of men, one of whom had been trying to jump out of the window.

In a later chapter we shall look at "the devil", but for now we note that for many people in covens all over the country, Satan is real. When Burns wrote *Tam o' Shanter* he was not making it all up, out of his imagination. The lass with the "cutty sark" was a real person, and the coven existed, as he tells in his letter accompanying the poem. The incident which inspired the poem may be fictitious, but the background is not. Burns, like Shakespeare, knew what he was writing about.

The awfulness of black witchcraft, emphasized recently by the revelation of rituals involving the abuse and even the death of children, must not lead us to the other extreme. This is what seems to have happened in previous generations, when the anti-witchcraft movement became as diabolic as the witchcraft.

We hardly need to spend time warning against black witchcraft, for both Charismatic and New Age Christians would abhor it. Yet there is also white witchcraft, and the New Age people do tend to veer towards it, so now we must look at this.

WHITE WITCHCRAFT

We have already looked at the word OCCULT, and noted that there may yet be much which is hidden from us, although Jesus tells us that there is nothing hidden which shall not be revealed. Though this is often taken to mean "The Last Judgement", this is not necessarily the limit of what he meant. Surely our Father means his children to explore the wonders of his Creation and to rejoice in them. That which is hidden, occult, today is meant to be shared new treasure tomorrow.

We come back to the point made earlier, that if there *are* powers and forces which Western science has not yet discovered, then learning to control them would bring about another real moral, spiritual crisis, for each new discovery does. Such discoveries in the hands of immature, unbalanced or twisted people would be even more dangerous at this level than nuclear power.

It is precisely such earth-forces which are spoken about by those who venture into this area, and they are very often very well-meaning people. If such forces are part of God's creation, then sooner or later humanity is meant to harness them to the glory of God. But if they are uncovered, as in the case of atomic power and of some psychological insights, by people who are not right with God at the spiritual level, then terrible harm may ensue, and mere good intentions are no guard against this. Some white witches, as publicized in the press, are charming and highly-motivated people, but one trembles for them.

81

THE LIFE-FORCE

One of the basic ideas underlying a lot of thinking in this area is: THE LIFE-FORCE. This, it is asserted, flows through the universe, and can be harnessed for good or for evil... for healing or for cursing. Often it is equated with the Chinese CHI and with the Indian PRANA. Perhaps there *is* a light-energy which flows, like electricity, but higher up the spectrum. After all this is the result of centuries of observation by wise men in many countries, and we would be foolish to write it off too lightly.

The mistake which can lead to real danger is when this life-force is equated with the Holy Spirit. *Chi* and *prana* it may be... the Holy Spirit it is not. This life-force is part of God's creation if it exists, not God himself. The Holy Spirit is God, who is love, in action in us. The Holy Spirit is personal in the sense one may grieve the Spirit, resist the Spirit, but one can never harness the Spirit... "The Spirit blows where it wills". We may open ourselves to God's Holy Spirit, and be guided to do his work, we cannot make the Holy Spirit work for us.

The danger of such a theological error is that the human being is exalting his position to the point where he controls God, or thinks he does. It is in order to do good, yes, but at the cost of "you will be like God himself" (the serpent in Genesis 3:5), which, as we have seen, is the basic temptation: the desire for power. The desire to be in control is a subtle twisting of the human vocation on earth (Gen 1:28), so near the truth, but so deadly.

If, then, we meet people who are exploring into these territories with good motives, it would be counter-productive to be hostile to them, as many charismatic Christians would be. There is more need to think through our faith, so that we can reach the deep point at which we can share it with them. This will certainly involve listening to them rather than talking at them. We may have to learn where *our* understanding of the faith and of the world needs to be enlarged, and to understand why such people of good-will have rejected Christianity as we know it, or, if they are Christians already, have felt the need to explore these areas.

If their motive is ego-tripping, or the love of power, then we have to realize that they are very dangerous people. One such was such a staunch supporter of her minister that she began "dealing with" any elder who opposed him. After several such elders had had car-crashes, accidents and strange illnesses, the minister had to make a stand, and this was not easy for she was much respected in the community. (Her involvement with witchcraft was not generally known.) He claimed the shielding of Christ for himself and for his congregation, confronted her, with much prayer backing, and bound her not to continue. She was last heard of in a mental hospital. Facing these issues is quite beyond the scope of normal "Churchianity", and as the above minister found, we are driven to take a lot of things in the Bible a lot more seriously than is usual. The result of this is a deepening of our ministry, as he also found. The only real answer is not argument, but to "outshine" the darkness by the Love of Christ. The "voltage" of the Light in us must be stronger than the voltage of darkness in the other side.

WITCH-HUNTS

As an example of how diabolic witch-hunters can be, there is a hill outside Forres, Morayshire, and any woman suspected of being a witch was placed in a spike-lined barrel and rolled down this hill. If she survived, then she must be a witch. Could anything be more devilish?

In Exodus 22:18 it says, "You must not allow a witch to live." That does not justify cruelty, even if we take it literally. As it is, we do not keep a number of the other commands in the Old Testament to the letter, and people would be justified in asking why we demanded that this one should be so kept, especially when we know that on one occasion Jesus refused to take part in stoning a woman whom the Old Testament law required should be stoned (John 8:1ff). Yet the old command does point to the gravity of the situation.

On the other hand we are bound to issue: **A HEALTH WARNING!**

We know well from history that when people start literal witch-hunts, very nasty aspects of their characters emerge. It seems as if "the other side scores a double" by tricking those who are meant to be the children of light into allowing themselves to be poisoned by fear and cruelty.

It is easy to attract unhealthy characters with a chip on their shoulders by any campaign or movement which is strongly ANTI-SOMETHING, whether it is witch-hunting, spiritual warfare, anti-Catholic, anti-Protestant, anti-homosexual... anti-anything! Those attracted will soon cause more bitterness and poison to circulate in society.

When people become obsessed with what they are AGAINST, they are as much on the side of evil as the people they oppose. Of course healthy Christians will be engaged in spiritual warfare, and may have to take a stand against some movement... but the main emphasis must always be on outshining the darkness by love and laughter, and not by the devil's methods!

MIND CONTROL

Before we say good-bye to witches black and white, there is a modern form of the craft which is heavily disguised. It may even go under the name of "management training"!

Here is a quotation from an advertisement for a book taken from a Self Development Magazine:

Learn the silent commands which positively force others to obey your will! Simply by standing or sitting in a certain position, by moving certain parts of your body in subtle ways, or by the other methods described in this book, you will find that you can project unspoken orders that must be obeyed. Unspoken orders that must be obeyed. Think what you could do with that power!"

There is much more to it, but that is enough to point to the truly diabolic trick that is being played. One can see that it is a modern version of Jesus' temptations in the wilderness. It feeds the desire for power *over* people, to enforce *my* will, to achieve *my* ends, and this is the ultimate sin. The person may think it involves good-will and good aims, but...!

Apparently there are firms which send members of staff on such courses to make them more efficient salesmen and so on. One can see that business-men who had truly learned mind-control by psychic means would indeed be formidable. Yet we know only too well from trying to help some such people, that after one or two initial successes, there seems to be confusion. People who thought that they had the power to rule the world (even as Satan offered Jesus), actually find themselves getting deeper and deeper into trouble, and of course bringing misery to many others, especially to those closest to them.

Having said all that, let us face it that many New Age people one meets are if anything much more gentle and less addicted to power over others than some Christians! **While there does seem to be this diabolic end of the New Age movement, it seems the very antithesis of what most ordinary New Agers think.**

CONCLUSIONS

Either:

* Those who write such books are consciously hoodwinking inadequate, gullible people.

Or:

* The writers have in fact discovered ways in which to use thought-control.

Either way, it is dangerous nonsense. As human beings made in the image of God we are indeed meant to harness the hidden powers in nature... in human nature as well as in "nature".

The Gospels, however, show how in Gods Creation, POWER must always be subject to LOVE. People were often amazed at Jesus' power, but it was always for OTHERS, never for himself. We see that Jesus would not even exert power *over* the twelve disciples closest to him, far less *over* the people who sought to kill him. Even at that fatal moment in the garden before his arrest, he was aware that he could call on more legions of angels than there were legions of Roman soldiers in Palestine. He resisted that temptation.

If even Jesus at such a point was tempted to use power *over* people, who are we to think that we would not be tempted in the same way?

It is quite plain from the accounts that the very-Christian witch-hunters, at whom we looked in the last section, enjoyed their power *over* the women brought before them, and were therefore, as we saw, moving on to the diabolic side.

However, lest we become over self-righteous, we have to confess that we have seen churches of various varieties and Charismatic fellowships in which the leader, pastor or whatever he was called, exerted a terrible power *over* those who joined. This is because in their styles of worship and pastoral care, without realising it, such leaders employ some of the very same techniques which no doubt would be found in the book about mind control. In truly spiritual worship, we are led to be open to God and to receive the Gifts of the Holy Spirit, which give the power to serve God and to help other people.

We owe it to well-meaning people - usually those who have been "losers" in life - who seek development in these ways, to be clear in our teaching. Such people are in real danger, unless they realize that their answer does not lie in seeking power. It lies in seeking LOVE, the

Love of God and true love for others, especially for those who have made them "losers".

Unfortunately not many congregations offer courses of truly spiritual development, yet it would seem that there is a real urgency to counter these diabolic traps by offering something better.

It was a famous politician who commented that **"power corrupts and absolute power corrupts absolutely."** Nowhere is that truer than of the psychic and spiritual spheres.

CASTING SPELLS

We are in real trouble with the next word *chavar* on our list, translated as using charms, or casting spells, for the Hebrew word means ONE WHO TIES KNOTS. So it would seem that our Scouts are going to join the pharmacists in outer darkness! It was a good thing that our translators did not translate literally, or our literally-minded brethren would have been tying themselves in knots!

It is all very puzzling: the translators are probably right, and there must have been some form of casting spells which involved tying knots. After all we talk of "spell-binding", so there must be some ancient folk memory even in this country which links spells and binding or knots. In fact I remember hearing a programme on the radio* a long time ago, in which a man told how he had seen an old woman up in Orkney tying knots in the bent-grass so that the ends were pointing to the neighbouring croft. She was singing or chanting a primitive version of the song, "I'll give you one-ho, green grow the rushes oh." He asked her what she was doing, and she explained that her neighbour had put a hex on her cow, and this was an anti-spell device. So there is some connection between knots and spells, and the witch was the expert in these things, although ordinary folk could learn them.

* Incidentally the same broadcast went on to say that there are versions of this song in many lands, in some cases with a phonetic similarity in certain verses. It seems to be left over from pre-Christian magical practices, christianized, and then trivialized to being a tongue-twister we enjoy singing.

BLESSING AND CURSING

The idea that you can subvert the life-force for destructive, malicious ends, or that you can enrol demonic elements to help you harm somebody, is obviously wrong. And as we have also already remarked, if people had learned from the experience of the past generations, they would have known that those who call in the earth-forces for "good" purposes, get far more than they bargain for. Called in as allies, they take over bit by bit.

Yet there is a lesson to be learned from the most common "spell": CURSING. Strangely enough most people know intuitively how to curse: storing up a "head of steam" of real venom, and then using all the verbal obscenities available to hurl this negative energy at the victim. Yet how often do we realize that the opposite is also true: blessing is when you get a good head of steam of love and goodness and express it verbally with all the verbal force that one can muster. It is a real power for good... in fact it is the fundamental act of Christian healing. Its effectiveness depends on how great a head of good steam one has stored up! How tragic it is when this great spiritual weapon, the Blessing, is gabbled through at the end of a service, as if it were just the sign that the service is ended.

Many of those familiar with Africa and such places can testify that the spells of witch-doctors are surprisingly effective. Our text, however, forbids us to attempt to channel the basic life-forces for selfish ends, or even for supposed good ends.

The basic principles here are:

* **If we are in tune with our Maker then the basic life-forces will be in tune with us.**

* **We must not use spells to invoke them to serve our ends.**

HYPNOSIS

Now we come to look at another form of treatment which is generally condemned in conservative Christian literature as being a form of "spell": HYPNOSIS. It may well be that some people who cast spells were in fact misusing hypnosis, but we cannot say, therefore all hypnosis comes under the heading of "spells".

The condemnation is usually based on the principle that no human being should surrender control of the mind to another. This is surely a right principle, and a very important one, although it is questionable if this is really what happens in well-conducted hypnotherapy.

To understand hypnotism we have to use a different picture of the human being from the one with which we began. We switch to

Jung's picture: a cone, with the conscious, rational mind at the peak, and beneath it the various levels of the subconscious mind. As generally understood in psychological terms, this subconscious is the FEELING aspect of us, it is not rational, but responds to beauty, or ugliness and so on. In it are our memories, some of which are so painful that they arouse emotions which we do not usually allow to the surface. After all it is not "polite" to show too much emotion! However these memories have their own ways of coming to the surface, for instance in dreams.

The adult conscious mind can to a large extent control the input into the subconscious, and also control what comes to the surface. When it cannot do so, we usually reckon that the person is "disturbed". We usually need skilled help if we are to face really painful inner traumas and deal with them. Hypnotherapy is one such way of helping.

What happens in hypnosis is that the conscious mind is lulled, so to speak, in order to allow the deeper consciousness to surface. In this way patient and therapist have access to the depths.

It is this access which gives rise to a fear that suggestions can be made which in a normal state, the patient would reject. However properly trained hypnotherapists would deny that there is this danger, and affirm, as do patients, that no such thing could happen. In fact even in deep hypnosis the patient can reject any suggestion which is contrary to his/her character.

PLAYING GOD?

Further hesitation is caused by a deep-rooted belief that none but the Spirit of God should have free access to the inner secrets of our hearts. It is on this understanding that many people condemn hypnosis.

But it is not as simple as that, after all what we call hypnosis is part of all religion, even if it does not go under that name! The technique is simple and universal: the repetition of phrases, the rhythmic beat, the focusing of attention. These result in a person being open to suggestion in a way that allows an input into the mind which might not be possible while full consciousness reigns.

One thinks here of the oriental mantra, the Roman Catholic rosary, the Orthodox "Jesus prayer", the repetitive choruses of the Charismatics, the "beat" at a disco, the chanting of the football crowd and so on. All these to some extent develop an ASC by a form of mild hypnosis. In fact from a psychological standpoint, most Christian worship is aimed at producing at least a low level of suggestibility, a mild hypnosis. Through singing and liturgy, either or both, the barriers between people go down, they are open to the flow of a common mind, and for the Christian this open-ness is preparation for the Holy Spirit.

To digress for a moment, it would appear that ordinary Church of Scotland worship is aimed at the conscious mind more than most, which is why young people who have experienced the ecstasy of hypnotic music and the mild hypnosis of being part of a disco or football crowd, find services so dull!

In terms of healing, what we call "the healing of memories" involves a lowering of the barriers so that the subconscious is being dealt with directly. As one reads Psalm 139, or focuses the imagination on Jesus, on a cross or a text such as "Be still and know that I am God", it would be very naive not to realize that one is using mild hypnosis. Sometimes it goes deeper, and we find the person "slain in the Spirit" or "resting in the Spirit". This is a quick way into a deep hypnotic state. However when this is a true work of the Spirit, the person is not conscious of his or her surroundings, and therefore not open to "suggestion". He/she is, however open to God.

Things go wrong when people who claim to be Christian healers begin, without realizing it, to depend on hidden psychological gimmicks. Then we find that those attending their meetings become obsessed with, for example, "slaying in the Spirit", so that it becomes just a psychological "trip" with a Christian flavour. The use of such hypnotic techniques can produce false conversions and healings, which wear off and leave the person in a worse state than ever. So while we respect the warning given by conservative Christians against hypnosis, we have also to ask them to recognise that very often their preachers and Christian counsellors are using these very techniques without realising it.

BONDAGE AND DEPENDENCY

The danger which we face is that when any of these techniques are used, be it by the preacher, the healer, or the hypnotherapist, it is very easy for a person to develop a dependency, or, even worse, find themselves in psychic bondage. Such *dependencies* have to be broken gently but firmly and then healthy, loving relationships must be formed to replace them. On the other hand *bondages* require the Word of Authority in Jesus' Name, and the re-orientation of the person's life.

Of course these problems can form in many ways, for example we find adults who are still in "bondage" to parents long dead and gone. We find people in bondage to their ministers, especially if the latter are strong personalities. In fact we have had experience of a number of people who needed to be freed from a bondage because they had been involved in the more extreme charismatic sects, house-churches etc. Yet those who use hypnotherapy would be clear that there is no more danger of this type of trouble arising during their treatment than there is in these other spheres. Often it is the patient's immaturity rather than the technique which lays him or her open to this.

Of course, the minister, hypnotherapist, or parent concerned would strongly deny having tried to create a bondage. The minister would think in terms of asking for a total commitment to the Lord's work, oblivious of the degree to which this implied submission to him as a person. In the same way parents who have left their children with a bondage would be sure that they had only done their duty to their children. As far as the hypnotherapist is concerned, therefore it is important that he or she be acting under supervision, as part of a team, including counsellors, so that others can spot dependencies etc. forming and step in. On this subject E.Jefferies comments:

> If the patient is directed in their healing through hypnosis, to depend upon the power of Jesus for healing, then the bonding, if any, is likely to be to him, and that is not a bad thing.

SO... let us agree that if the hypnotherapist brings people into a bondage situation, he is very far wrong, but that this is not necessarily the case in all hypnotherapy. I have myself recently interviewed two people who have received treatment from Christian hypnotherapists, one of whom was Esmond Jefferies, referred to in the last paragraph. They confirmed what I had gathered from many other less specific conversations: that while under hypnosis they were *more* aware, not less.

A CASE STUDY

On one occasion I was present while Mr Jefferies was giving treatment, and was able to observe this myself. The Lord Jesus was immediately called on and the patient was directed to him.

In the other case, on enquiry from both therapist and patient it was clear that the only difference between what this hypnotherapist was doing, and what is done in "the healing of memories" was that the religious element was less obvious, although it was still done in a Christian setting.

In both cases after the treatment the patient claimed to have been in control sufficiently to be aware of all that was going on, and able to reject anything which seemed wrong. In both cases the hypnotherapy was only part of the treatment, counselling also took place, and in one of the cases the laying-on of hands for physical ailments was also given.

In one case the centre offered ordinary prayer, Bible-study and worship to follow on what had been done, also encouraging people to attend their own churches if possible.

I would have to say that in these cases I felt that there was no bondage being formed, that the personality of the patient was respected... perhaps more so than in some "religious" forms of treatment!

Nevertheless, people who are looking for "power" can find the idea of being a hypnotist attractive, and this is very dangerous. The desire for power over people for its own sake always leads to disaster. That is where the Old Enemy very definitely comes in!

ANAESTHESIA

One aspect we have overlooked so far, is that hypnosis is used where ordinary anaesthetics are not suitable, perhaps because the patient is allergic to them. In child-birth, in dentistry and in ordinary operations it is possible to use hypnosis.

Now I would ask the reader a question: if you had to have an operation, and were offered the choice between a general anaesthetic and hypnosis by a person such as one of the above, which would you choose? Or take the question even further: if you were to have dental surgery, and were told that your heart could not stand the anaesthetic, would you choose hypnosis or facing the operation fully conscious?

In deciding this, one has to face the fact that we do not know the effect on the psyche of drugs which knock us out. The doctors do not usually ask about the psychic effects of the drugs they give. We do not know much about the ASC under anaesthetics. Remember the case quoted earlier in which the person under anaesthetic was aware of the conversation in the theatre. This would seem to be yet another case of people questioning anything which they feel is labelled "alternative", while at the same time meekly accepting whatever the medical profession says.

We have to point out a danger of a very mild use of anaesthesia by hypnosis: one can use mild hypnotism to convince people that they do not suffer from diseases of the mind or of the body, when they do in fact suffer from them. For instance, an overwhelming personality can tell a suggestible person: "You are not suffering from pain". This may may cut off the pain but leave the disease. The result may be disastrous. This happens in some of the less desirable "healing services".

91

CONCLUSIONS

Hypnosis is an altered state of consciousness, mild forms of which are part of everyday life. In this state we are more suggestible, more open to our psychic environment.

* It can be used to help people discover hidden hurts and problems.

* It can also be used as an anaesthetic.

* Opening up a mind under hypnosis is as drastic as opening up a body for an operation. It should only be done when really necessary, when treatment via the conscious mind has failed.

* It should only be used by properly qualified and supervised people. One should check with anyone who claims to be a hypnotherapist to see if he/she is a member of the British Society of Medical and Dental Hypnosis.

Hypnosis is dangerous if used as a form of entertainment or as a way of getting power over people. The main danger is of bondages forming. If there is any psychic uncleanness in the therapist, any spiritual darkness, then there is a real danger of infection.

There is, perhaps, more danger in the use of these techniques by people who do not realize that they are using them, than in the frank use of them. One should certainly never submit to even the mildest hypnotism by somebody with whom one is not entirely "at home" spiritually. There must be a real empathy.

When using hypnosis at any level we must be careful, on our guard against the old Distorter, taking precautions. *From the therapist's side:* there must be prayerful preparation and follow-up, surrendering the patient to God. *From the patient's side:* there must be a re-affirming the Lordship of Christ alone in the soul.

THE INNER SANCTUARY

The inner sanctuary of the human soul is "holy ground" and we do right to defend it against meddlers of any description. This includes well-meaning Christian people who have read a book or two about inner healing! Our inmost being is to be opened to the Holy Spirit, and to that Spirit alone. Any who violate that principle, even if it is under the best supposed Christian guises, are doing grave wrong. Only with

92

great reverence and respect should we start exploring another's inner sanctuary. In Christian prayer together (as for instance when ministry is being given to somebody), and in worship, some of these techniques come naturally, flowing from the Spirit. But God never forces His Way into our lives. Therefore there must be no forcing an entrance into the sub-conscious.

10 THE LIVING AND THE DEAD

CONTACTING THE DEAD

The last three items on the "forbidden" list all seem to relate to the dead. The first two both refer to something which a person *has*, not to something one *does*. They are literally, "he who has an *ob* or a *yiddeoni*". The first is translated "he who hath a familiar spirit" in the Authorized version, and so "medium" in the RSV, and "consults ghosts" in the Jerusalem Bible. The second one is translated "wizard" in the RSV, "spiritualist" in the New International Version (NIV), and the Jerusalem Bible just adds "and spirits" to the foregoing phrase. This chapter brings us face to face with not only spiritualism but with the New Age version of it: channelling. The third and last item is necromancy. *Those not interested in biblical meanings may want to skip the next 5 paragraphs.*

OBS AND ENDS

"He who has an *ob*"... a what? An OB. But what is an *OB*? Nobody knows, but there are a number of references to people having them: Lev 19:31, 20:27, Isa 28:3. In Job 32:19 it refers obviously to a wineskin, so there is a suggestion of something hollow, perhaps a cave or hollow statue. One thinks here of the Iliad, when Ulysses consulted Achilles' spirit in the cave, the site of which has recently been discovered. This fits the story in 1 Sam 28:7, "a woman who has an *ob*", for it goes on to say that Samuel rose out of the earth. In Isaiah 29:4 it seems to suggest that whatever it was spoke with a twittering voice, which does not fit the Samuel story. On the other hand in Ezekiel's design for the Temple (41:26) we find that the siderooms off the sanctuary "have *obs*", translated "thick planks" in the AV and "overhangs" in the NIV. So the Temple "has an *ob*", in fact several! Perhaps it is "wineskins" in this case. Whatever the meaning, it does often seem to suggest some link with the dead, especially taking into account the story of Saul, so perhaps "medium" is a reasonable modern translation. However its exact meaning is not *ob*vious!

Now we look at the phrase which is translated as "a spiritualist"... the Hebrew *yiddeoni* and the phrase is literally "he who has a knowing one". It would seem to be a way of getting information from the dead. In Isaiah 8:19 it seems to be linked with twittering, bird-like noises, again like an ob. Could it be a mummified bird? Whatever it is, Isaiah thinks it a foolish way to make political decisions, one should rather seek the Living God. The phrase "a knowing one" describes rather well the spirits which New Age people speak about when they refer to channelling.

Whatever *obs* and *yiddeonis* were, it would seem that they were part of the spiritualist's equipment, such as an ouija board today. They were ways of communicating with the dead in order to get guidance as to what to do. Note that what is referred to in the Bible concerns decision-making; there is no idea of trying to establish whether there is life beyond death, and no question of what today we call "psychic research". We have to work out the guide-lines ourselves.

NECROMANCY

On the surface this looks like a repeat of the previous two items, so we deal with it now to get it out of the way! In most translations it is hard to see where the difference is, but actually necromancy meant reading the omens in dead bodies. A number of translations get this wrong. We have already referred to the passage in Ezekiel in which the king cast arrows *and spread the liver*. It is not said whether the liver belonged to some wretched subject, or whether it was an animal's. But this was common practice, in fact dead bodies were kept for this purpose. Those who know Burns' *Tam O'Shanter* will remember that the witches' dance was surrounded by open coffins and various other dead bodies. Burns knew what he was talking about! Even today we occasionally read of graveyards violated because somebody has been indulging in necromancy. However, it is not likely that anybody in either the New Age movement or the Charismatic movement will indulge in necromancy, and it is so obviously perverted that we will spend no more time on it.

CONSULTING THE DEAD

With regard to consulting the dead we are again in surprising territory. For the Old Testament, which was the "Bible" for Jesus and the apostles, has very little teaching about life after death, in fact the Sadduccees of Jesus' day maintained that the main part of it, the first five books, had no reference to anything beyond this life. The promise to Abraham and to David was not of eternal life, but of generations to come in this world. Other religions made elaborate rituals for the dead, while the Jews did not. Yet in spite of this lack of Biblical reference to life after death there are all these prohibitions about consulting the dead through *obs* and *yiddeonis*!

With the Old Testament prophets, we are clear that we should not "consult the dead on behalf of the living" (Isaiah 8:19). As we explore the reasons for this prohibition, we must remember two guiding principles already stated:

* **The higher up the spectrum one goes, the more subtle become the temptations.**

* **The most subtle, destructive temptations always appear as angels of light.**

A PLAUSIBLE ARGUMENT

Why should people want to consult "spirit guides"? One person explained it like this: "We do not go to the Queen every week for our pensions, we expect to get them from one of her lower officials. If we go to a bank, we do not expect to see the manager every time, but we do our normal transactions with the person behind the counter. In the same way, we deal normally with our guides, not God."

A plausible parable, but it misses the point of the Gospel which is that it is precisely this intimate relationship with God for every day which is offered!

MEDIUMS

The first thing which the Church objects to is the role of the medium. The word "medium" means "the thing in the middle". In 1 Timothy 2:5 we find the statement that "there is one mediator between God and men: Jesus Christ." It is the same basic word, except that here it is masculine, whereas "medium" is neuter. It means: MIDDLE-MAN. In Hebrews 8:6, 9:15, 12:24, again Jesus is referred to as *THE* Middle-man forging the New Covenant between God and humanity. We are therefore uneasy about anybody who seems to be claiming to be the medium through which human beings can contact "the beyond", however one envisages it.

Now there are spiritualists who claim to be Christian and who would agree that Jesus is *the* mediator between God and ourselves; but they would allow that mediums are links with the spirits of the dead. The Gospel is, however, that through Jesus we become aware of the Kingdom of God, and that being born again by water and the Spirit, we enter the Kingdom of God (John 3:5). It is as we grow in the New Life that we become aware of levels of life and of love which natural man cannot glimpse. In our prayer life and in our worship we may be able to partake, as many in the Bible did, with the worship in the heavenly places. We become aware of the "great cloud of witnesses surrounding us" (Hebrews 12:1). In worship we are to ascend to where "they" are, we are not to try to bring them back down to our level.

When, instead of growing in the spirit, people try to take a short cut to the spiritual through the medium of somebody else's psychic gifts, something has gone wrong. Of course the wrong may be with the church... if the preacher is only concerned with promoting his religious organization, or with social justice, or with converting individuals, then the seeking soul may look elsewhere for the reality of the spiritual, and for the explanation of the psychic.

We must realise too, that even if the voices of the dead thus called up are genuine, and not demonic imitations as some Christians maintain, there is no real guarantee that they are really any better or wiser than us. Neither can we be sure that their motives are any purer. They may know some things which are not known to us, but there is very little knowledge coming from them which is truly enlightening. Sometimes specific information is surprisingly correct, sometimes wildly wrong. There are many cases of people whose "channelling" has been shown to be genuine, yet who have finished up deluding and deluded. The great American "Valiantine"* was one such. It is hardly surprising that to *depend* on such for guidance in worldly matters is consistently forbidden.

*Valiantine was one of the great mediums or channels of this century. For instance one day he produced a voice speaking a strange language which somebody thought sounded like Chinese; they brought in a professor of Oriental studies who said something like this: "He is speaking old classical Chinese, and there are only three people in the West who could understand it, and I am one of them. He claims to be Con Fu Tse (Confucius)." The professor then proceeded to discuss some of the doubtful areas in the text of the old manuscripts. He was sure that it must be Con Fu Tse himself! Such phenomena were very convincing. Yet later Valiantine went in for materialisations; his friends set up experiments to prove that he could - only to prove that he was cheating. The only possible conclusions are:

(1)   The "spirits" did not know about the checks, even though their voices were in the room.

(2)   They knew, but could not warn Valiantine.

(3)   They knew but did not warn him, playing the Devil's favourite game of boosting a person up to the heights, then crushing him cruelly.

TRANCE

Now we look at another feature of the spiritualist scene: trance. A feature of the *seance* is that one person goes into a trance, and that all present must be in some sense in tune with the person in trance. This is an ASC in which as we have seen, the psyche lies open and can receive communication directly from another, without going through the senses. It is not, however, confined to spiritualists. For instance, we read in Acts 10:10 that Peter fell into a trance during his time of prayer, and received specific instructions from God through a vision. Typically, when this sort of visionary, specific guidance is given to St Peter, it is because he is to be asked to do something which would go right against his whole religious conviction, something his common sense could never handle on its own. Such an experience (of guidance in a trance) is not the normal Christian experience, as a further reading of Acts shows.

Paul, in 2 Corinthians 12, also speaks of an experience which was obviously "trance", as was St John's state at the beginning of the book of Revelation. It would seem in these cases that the trance was the work of the Spirit, and not the deliberate use of a technique to get an ASC. The focus of attention in each case was the Lord himself.

For the Christian, the body is the TEMPLE OF THE HOLY SPIRIT (1 Cor 6:19), and while it is is made in such a way that trance can be induced (eg by methods of breathing), this is not for deliberate use. The gateway to our consciousness must be surrendered to none but the Holy Spirit. However high-sounding the "spirits" contacted, they should not be allowed to take over the Temple of the Holy Spirit, to speak through our mouths or to blot out our consciousness.

SENSITIVES

In such circles we also find such people who are referred to as "sensitives" rather than "mediums". They do not necessarily work in terms of *seances* and trances. Having a "thin psychic skin", they claim to be able to pass messages from one level of being to another. While not claiming to be a medium, such a person easily becomes the focus of attention, to be consulted when decisions are to be made. Anyone with this natural sensitivity is subject to subtle temptations, and is "at risk" in many ways; as we have seen, there is evil at every level, so it only requires a little slip for the sensitive to be deceived disastrously.

CHANNELLING

The New Age version of this is known as CHANNELLING, and the basic idea is that one learns to be guided by some higher spirit. New Age channelling concentrates more on "do-it-yourself" and less on special mediums, though of course there are the "big names" in channelling too. In *Healing with Love*, Dr Harold Laskow begins by referring to his "dear friends Lazaris and Poonaji", both of them spirit guides. He expresses gratitude for all they have taught him, and he says that the first step in such healing is to become aware of your own spirit guides. Much that he says in the book is interesting and valuable, yet its reference to God and to Jesus fall far short of the glory of the Gospel.

SAINTS AND ANGELS

Now of course the Lord does refer to guardian angels, and the angel Gabriel comes into the Bible at various points. Throughout the history of the Church people have had visions which involved some the "saints departed". Not least, we learn that the Lord himself communed with Moses and Elijah on the Mount of Transfiguration.

Hebrews 12:1 compares our situation with that of athletes on the field surrounded by a great crowd of onlookers, those who ran the race before us. Some Christians do become vividly aware of this when they pray. Three examples:

(1) St Brigida of Sweden who recorded her revelations, mostly from the Virgin Mary, but she also met with St Francis who had died before her time.

(2) The great 20th century Sikh Christian Sundar Singh was aware of communion with individuals in the "great crowd of witnesses" as well as with the Lord himself.

(3) C.S.Lewis appeared to J.B.Phillips in the depths of depression and helped him (see Phillips' book *Ring of Truth*.) This was not sought, but it was a gift from God. Most of us know of similar instances. This is very different from what is prohibited: going to somebody who is "psychic" in order to call somebody up.

*   **If God in His Wisdom decides to communicate with us through an angel or through somebody who has died, that is his prerogative. We are not to seek to bring them "back down".**

Christians are not unfamiliar, then, with guardian angels and with the saints departed. In fact many of our hymns invoke their help in worship. As on a sports field, it is good to know that you have people shouting for you in the crowd! But you must keep your eye on the finishing tape. So the writer of Hebrews tells us that we must keep our eyes on Jesus, the Starter and the Finisher of our race (in those days it was the hand of the Finisher which served where we have a tape).

Preoccupation with saints, angels, spirit guides and the like can provide a false spirituality, a substitute for a living relationship with God through Jesus Christ in the fellowship of the Holy Spirit.

* **In a properly focused life, saints and angels will be there as needed, but they are never to be the main focus of our prayer.**

CHANNELLING AND PROPHECY

There are, of course, strong similarities between people who have developed "spirit guides" and what Charismatic groups experience when they have somebody in the fellowship with the gift of prophecy or of knowledge. In fact some people I know who had once been involved with spiritualism, went to a meeting in a Charismatic Church at which the guest worked by the Word of Knowledge. They commented that it was incredibly similar to what happens when a visiting medium comes in spiritualist circles.

In a Charismatic setting the person claims that any message or knowledge comes from God through the Holy Spirit. In a New Age setting the person claims to be channelling a higher spirit. In both settings there is the same danger for the people taking part: they tend to form a dependency on the person with the gift. And in both settings there is the same danger for the person with the gift: he/she very soon finds that the gift gives power *over* people, and then there is the devil to pay.

Make no mistake: even the Gifts of the Holy Spirit can be misused to give a person power over others; they come to be consulted on all decisions, even though the request is in the form of wanting to know the will of God. Yet seldom is the person with this gift also given the gift of leadership, administration and understanding, and therefore if the gift gives them too much prominence in the community, there will be trouble. Those who remember the story of Saul in the Bible will remember that people were horrified that their King was among the prophets. They had every reason to be! The prophet and the seer (see-er) have their places, but not as the leader of the community; she (it is often a she) needs the caring discipline of the community, and the community needs to be disciplined enough not to refer to her too much.

We see then, that often the person with a gift of Prophecy starts becoming the group's medium, even though they may claim to be very anti-spiritualist, anti-New Age. That is why any truly Christian group must never become preoccupied with "the gifts" of any one person. The command is to look outward, preach the gospel, heal the sick; focus on the reality and need of the world around. It may be that sometimes the Lord may want to give specific instructions through someone with the gift of Prophecy, and that is as it should be; but it is only too easy for groups to get hung up on "the gifts" so that they degenerate into something very different from a Christian Church.

This is what had happened at Corinth. The famous chapter on LOVE (1 Corinthians 13), read in its context, with the previous and following chapters, shows a situation which is only too familiar in the Charismatic Movement today.

Therefore, while we warn against spiritualist mediums and channels, we must beware of falling into the same trap ourselves. **Whenever the focus of attention is on somebody's "spiritual gift", and the life of the group becomes dependent upon it, look out for trouble.**

CONCLUSIONS

* **God may use any part of His Creation, including the "spirits of the departed" or angels to contact us, but we are to focus on Him alone.**

* **Our bodies are Temples of the Holy Spirit and are not to be opened to any other.**

* **In our prayer-life God may use trance to communicate with us, but our focus in prayer must be on loving communion with Him, not on our own states of consciousness.**

* **God has created some people "sensitives", but their place in the community must never be allowed to be central. Indeed**

they have a special need to be part of a community concerned to work out the total Christian life.

* **Such natural "sensitives" must offer up this gift, like any other gift, so that it is surrendered to God, and never regarded as personal property.** Natural sensitivity must be converted to sensitivity to the Holy Spirit, and if this is the case, the person will only be aware of evil if the Spirit allows it in order to bring light to those in darkness.

* **There should be a place in Christian worship during which God may speak directly to us through somebody with the gift of Prophecy, and not just through sermons.** The lack of the sense of immediacy and of expectation may indeed drive people to seek it elsewhere.

* **Any prophecy or word of knowledge must always be cross-checked by the community, and related to basic biblical teaching.**

* **In our prayers and worship we are to rise up to communion with the "great cloud of witnesses who surround us" (Hebrews 12:1) and not try to bring them back down to earth.**

Part III: ON CLOSER EXAMINATION

We now turn to some more general issues, using the insights which we have gained so far. Not everybody is interested in going into each subject more deeply, so a bit of judicious skipping is recommended for those who are not used to theological reading! However even if you do find this section a bit heavy, please do not give up before reading the final chapter.

11 THE WORLD AND ITS SECRETS

PLANET EARTH

It is in their attitude to the world that New Age and Charismatic Christians are divided most clearly. For the New Ager this planet is a living organism, a unity, of which we human beings are a part. They see this organism as made up of many beings and energies, all interlinked.

What life is about... and therefore what religion and morality are about... as far as New Agers are concerned, is our relationship to this living organism. "Talking to plants" is just one manifestation of this attitude which has caught public attention, perhaps because many people do it naturally. Christians have always maintained that a right relationship with other *human beings* is the essence of morality, and God's prime concern. What is new is the insight that this does not go far enough, we are to relate positively to the whole organism which is this planet.

On the other hand in most charismatic services there is very little reference to the earth and its creatures as such. There may be a reference to the beauty of the earth in a hymn, but little sense of the planet being more than the scenery in which human life is lived. Extreme charismatics teach that the earth is Satan's*: it will soon be destroyed by fire anyway. Such people see conservation and the "green" movement as satanic. However we must not judge all charismatics by their extremists any more than we judge the New Age by *their* extremists!

*This understanding is based upon verses such as 1 John 5:19. The NIV translates it: "The whole world is under the control of the evil one", and other versions are much the same. The Greek is literally: "The whole *kosmos* lies in the evil". The word *kosmos* means "set-up" and in terms of somebody writing in the Roman Empire, as St John was, it meant "the Roman establishment", and that empire was certainly wallowing in evil at that time! *Kosmos* is NOT the word which refers to the earth, which is *ge*. Sometimes *kosmos* is used to mean "everybody", like the French *tout le monde*, as in John 3:16 "God so loved the *kosmos*"... It does not mean "the cosmos" as we use the word today. So there is no justification for writing off the earth as Satan's.

The Christian bases his/her understanding on firm Biblical teaching:

* **In the first chapters of Genesis, earth is seen to be affected by human sin.**

* **In the Psalms (e.g. 96 & 98) nature is invited to rejoice with us at the coming of the Lord.**

* **In Hosea 2 God offers a new covenant which includes the whole of creation.**

* **In Isaiah 11 we have the picture of nature's harmony restored.**

* **In Romans 8 nature is seen groaning and travailing waiting for the sons of God to come into their own.**

* **In the Benedicite, an old hymn from the apocrypha, we call on the whole of creation to join us in praising God.**

We see, then, a firm Biblical basis for treating the earth as a responsive part of God's Creation, even if over the centuries this aspect has been rather neglected, and treated as something "merely poetic", and not to be taken literally (it is always interesting to note what "fundamentalists" who think they take the Bible literally, actually do not take literally!)

GOD OR GAIA?

The more extreme New Agers see the earth itself as God, worshipping the creation rather than the Creator, as St Paul put it. They often go so far as to re-introduce the mother-goddess Gaia. This, the Greek version of the earth-mother, is popular with feminists as a way of getting away from a male God. However the Biblical prophets were very familiar with earth-mother goddesses ("the earth-mother who devours her children"), and what their worship led to! Even then people found the fertility rites associated with the earth-mother and the sky-father much more fun than a God who was concerned with justice. The prophets, however, saw that the long-term results were disastrous, and usually led to human sacrifices, especially child-sacrifices.

On the other hand perhaps we can understand people feeling that they need more than an idea; they want a figure to personify the fact that we have to treat earth and its creatures with respect, and to avoid the rape of earth which we have witnessed. If people are turning to Gaia again, perhaps Christians should look again at what they have been saying, or NOT saying, about our relationship to earth!

Yet it remains true that we have to worship the Creator alone, and while there may or may not be beings at a lower level, we are meant to enter into our inheritance as children of God, a status high above the nature forces, such as Gaia or Pan... another nature god popular in some places. The principle we worked out earlier in the book applies here too:

If we are right with Our Father then the natural forces will be in harmony beneath us, and will work out his purposes for us.

When we get it wrong, and forces which are meant to be below us are allowed to be the focus of worship and attention, the balance of nature is upset. If, instead of loving and caring for God's good earth, we begin to worship the "the earth-mother who devours her children", eventually the rites associated with such worship develop terrifying features, even if they begin as gentle nature worship.

Let us now return:

* to the ordinary person who has become aware of the wrong-ness of the usual attitude to the earth;

* to the person troubled by the threatened extinction of whales and dolphins;

* to the person horrified at the destruction of the rain-forests;

* to the person who feels that some farming methods are an offence against nature;

* to the person who has a real "feeling" for plants and animals.

If people feel such things, surely this is the sign of a moving of God's Spirit within them. However, few churches would offer worship which would lead this moving of the Spirit into a full flowering. Further among the list of the activities in most congregations, there is very rarely a group which has concern for the earth as its focal point Therefore people who are moved to penitence and action by what is happening to the earth tend to look elsewhere. Yet such an awareness should lead to a real turning to the Creator in penitence for what we are doing to his world, and in prayer for help to heal the earth. God knows we need the Holy Spirit if we are to tackle this enormous problem!

A congregation which is really showing such a biblical concern for the earth and its creatures will feel a natural affinity with all who are concerned with "green" issues, and will draw some into the total life of Christ. At the same time, the church's wider concerns should ensure that those concerned with particular issues do not go to fanatical extremes. Keep the balance.

STOICHEIA: ELEMENTAL SPIRITS

Thinking about the earth as an organism made up of many beings and energies, brings us to looking at the *stoicheia*. These odd characters have crept into this book several times already; they came very near the surface in the last section when we mentioned Pan and Gaia. It comes to us in a roundabout way as STOICAL. Therefore it is time to look them in the face, so to speak. The word comes into the New Testament 3 times. In one case, in Hebrews 5:12, the New English Bible translates it well as "the ABC of the faith." In Galatians 4 St Paul speaks of how, until Jesus came, they were in slavery to the *stoicheia*, whereas as now we can know God as "Abba, Father". In Colossians 2:8 & 20, however, amazement is expressed that people who had known the liberty and love of the Gospel should have fallen back on practices which subjected them to the *stoicheia*.

Now in Colossians one is very aware of many levels of unseen beings, of which the *stoicheia* are the lowest level. It is made quite plain that every level of unseen being is under the authority of Jesus the Christ, and therefore undue preoccupation with them is to miss the point. Our fellowship is with the Lord of all, and his underlings will serve us if we are in tune with him.

The *stoicheia* are sometimes called "elemental spirits". (They may not be "spirit" in the sense in which we are using the word in this book, but one has to bow to common usage!) People were once very aware of these spirits: earth spirits (mother earth), plant spirits (fairies), rock and mountain spirits (gnomes), and so on. What went wrong was that people began giving honour to these instead of to the Creator, and the result was disaster. It meant that natural order was upset, because humanity was meant to be OVER these beings not beneath them. They were not meant to be involved in human affairs.

Of course moderns find it hard to make sense of such talk, and if it just seems so much nonsense, then skip the rest of this section. But notice that humanity is getting itself into an awful mess because it is treating "the world as its oyster" with no reverence or regard to "nature". Many "primitive" people are warning us of the disaster to which the modern outlook on nature is heading. Perhaps we have de-personalised things too much!

If, however, you have talked to your plants, or have felt that some places welcomed you and some did not, then read on. If one concedes that there are such elementals, and that they have a place, then one has to ask what their place is. **Their concern is fertility**. There is no moral issue involved in the "propagation of the species" among plants and animals, but there is when it comes to human beings. If we "open the door" to communion with these beings, let alone make them our gods, then their fertility-concern becomes tangled up with human sexuality. The result is the sort of fertility cult which the prophets of Israel opposed, and which has emerged again in our day, when all sorts of terrible practices take place, and the *stoicheia* are perverted by human sin.

A farmer, a profound Christian, mentioned to me in the passing that of course trees, especially old trees, have a lot of spare *mana* which they will share with you if you ask them, for instance if you are very tired. However, he added: "You've to be careful of course".

Thinking later about what he had said, I remembered a case we had to deal with in which a family had become involved with a tree-worshipping, druid-type cult. What had seemed a happy heathen activity had taken a nasty turn sexually, and the family needed to get out; they found it was not easy to do so. This brings us back to a basic principle: if we upset the order of creation in this way, we find that it is not long before the old devil has his foot in the door!

We have to see that our function as the Children of God is to lead the creation's worship, not to worship nature.

It is part of the consciousness of this age in which we live, that we Europeans have been far too insensitive to the earth and all its creatures. We have to admit that our version of Christianity has failed to counter the view that anything which makes money is OK. In fact often by converting nations to Christianity we have made them as insensitive to the earth as we are, and have destroyed ecologically sound ways of living. That is the shame of the church. Now we must re-think... that, as we have seen, is the meaning of REPENT.

To focus this, look at the Pygmies, living in the forests of Africa. They speak of their Father the Forest in ways that seem strangely familiar to us, and before they hunt for food in it, they give the Forest a present, so that they GIVE as well as RECEIVE. Compare that with some of the White hunters who hunt for fun or money with little thought of the environment! Or, even worse, with the multi-national company which tears down the forest. Dare we say that these Pygmies are pagan and superstitious, needing "conversion" by European missionaries, while the whites concerned, some of whom are probably church members, are Christian and superior?

PROGRESS?

Mention of the Pygmies brings us to a point which needs to be thought through. If you read books about "aboriginal" people in various places, for instance in Australia, or the Kalahari bushmen, you will find that the *stoicheia* are very real to them. They take telepathy, dowsing and many other such strange phenomena for granted. They really do communicate with what we call "nature".

With the growth of Western science, we have tended to write off such views as quaint or even mad, because they do not see things as we do... and we, of course, are the sane ones, are we not? Our Western understanding, as many of us were taught in studies of the "development of religion", went something like this:

> Primitive man in his ignorance thought that everything was alive, as a young child thinks her doll is alive. Next he took to imagining that natural objects had spirits. Then he calculated that there must be a chief of the animal spirits, chief of the water spirits and so on. Thus he arrived at the Animal God (Celtic *Cernunnos*), and the Water God (Neptune). Finally, along came Moses proclaiming that there was only ONE God. This monotheism was the result of an evolution of religion.

However talking with people who have had experience of these people, and reading a few books soon leads one to different conclusions. It begins to look as if orginally, and in our "contemporary ancestors", there is an underlying awareness of the One God, and that the situation such as we find it in Rome, Greece and among the Celts of 2,000 years ago was a declension from that awareness of One-ness.

In what the aborigines call "dream time" there is a real communication with the *stoicheia*, and they are not hallucinating. It seems plain that there is more than primitive imagination involved. The people who have got to know these societies are sure that they are indeed sensitive to the living-ness of nature in a way that we are not. It appears that "dream time" involves a different state of consciousness.

Rudolf Steiner makes the point that it was necessary for humanity to move beyond this beautiful but naive state, and to learn to use the intellectual faculty with which humanity was endowed. So the long process of learning to think analytically began, leaving behind dream time as humanity began to explore the possibilities of the brain. This meant losing dream time slowly as more advanced levels of human activity opened up.

Naturally some individuals moved quicker than others, and the same with societies. In fact some communities are still in the "Eden" state today. However as the dream time faded, those individuals who still kept the awareness became the shamans, the witch-doctors, the priests. Religion as we know it formed. Temples were built, and surely such effort was not made, as we were told once, as massive confidence tricks! Some psychic phenomena must have really happened there.

Rituals were developed, often using hypnotic dances or hallucinogenic drugs to help the tribes as a whole to contact the *stoicheia*. Myths embodying the basic truths, were passed down. People tried to picture or model what was known of the *stoicheia*. So the whole gamut of religion emerged, but the original sensitivity was lost.

So the process went on, forcing humanity to "grow up", and if we follow that train of thought, we can see the parallel in family life: the children have to lose their innocent baby-relationship with parents, painfully on both sides, hoping that eventually a new, adult relationship will form which is deeper than the dream time of early childhood. So God wants adult children who work with Him, not spiritual babes.

DEVELOPING CONSCIOUSNESS

Many modern New Agers seem to regard the more intuitive state of consciousness as the next step forward for the human race, often identifying it with one side of the brain (a more doubtful proposition than many New Age books imply), and/or with the feminine in our nature and so on.

However it is plain from history that communities who work on this level cannot stand up to more developed cultures. Those who know them speak of the high level of morality such communities have, as well as how ecologically wise they are. Yet faced with the impact of western civilization they are helpless. In the case of the Kalahari bushmen they were even helpless in the face of the Bantu. Their contact with the *stoicheia* does not prove effective to safeguard their simple state of life.

I had a nurse in my congregation who had done a tour in Malaysia with the army. As a side-interest she had developed contact with an aboriginal tribe deep in the forest. She found that they were dying out for lack of vitamin C, and she used to treat them with "white man's magic". On one occasion when she was visiting them, they told her that she could not do her magic that day because it was their fire ceremony. They showed her their fire pit, and it was so hot that she could hardly get near enough to take a photo... I saw the photos which she DID take. The whole community, having been duly prepared, walked through the pit. One woman stumbled and fell, receiving minor burns.

This group, like the others we have mentioned, for all their psychic awareness, and strange powers at one level, are powerless at another. One may remember that in Britain, when the Romans became annoyed with the nationalistic attitude of the Druids, the legions marched up and massacred the lot in Anglesey while they were holding their "General Assembly". For all the much vaunted power of the Druids, they too were powerless faced with the calculating intellectual power of the Romans.

The lesson of history is that people who focus on psychic awareness, intuition, and on contact with the *stoicheia*, are overtaken by those who use intellectual, analytical thinking. We have to conclude that many New Age people are making a bad mistake if they think that developing the intuitive, feminine side and so on, is the way forward through which humanity can be saved. It is in fact a regression, and while we western nations do have to learn to be more intuitive, it is not the answer to our problems. It is all a matter of balance, as the Chinese would say.

IMPLICATIONS

Perhaps we Christians, even the more fundamentalist ones, are more affected by 19th century materialism than we realize. Perhaps the New Agers who insist that the world is a living organism, inter-acting at many levels, are saying something which needs to be said lest we deaden the planet. So let us come back to see what place the *stoicheia* might have in our lives.

The *first* point, which we have already hinted at, is that they have their own sphere, and humanity should cooperate with them in that sphere. We thought of this when we were considering herbalism. What is wrong is when we seek to involve them in human concerns, which is what people do in witch-craft and such-like.

Second, we should remember that of old the Church had two festivals that should help us to fulfil our function with regard to the earth forces: Rogation and Harvest. The first was concerned with blessing the newly sown seed in the fields, and each field received a blessing. It was a great enjoyable community occasion, and took quite a time. Now this seems meaningless to us with our materialistic view of nature, and it has dropped out of our church-life, and of community life.

We still have Harvest Festivals, but they have very often become little more than occasions when the children come to church, and they are usually just further occasions to publicize Christian Aid and the like. We have lost the true meaning of this festival.

Both these festivals which relate us to the earth, have to be recovered; they must really say something about our relationship to a nature which is able to respond in its own way to a true spirituality, yet which can be polluted and deadened by being treated wrongly by humanity. The *stoicheia* need us to lead them in worship, for we are "kings and priests" (to rule and lead in worship) for the creation.

Third, we can begin to take Psalms such as 96 & 98, and the great old canticles such as the Benedicite more seriously, and not dismiss them as mere poetic licence. Using them in our gardens or in the country-side might be more meaningful than we think.

While it is asking a lot to expect the church to change overnight in these matters, we ourselves can begin by relating more positively to the sections of the earth which we know. "Talking to plants" is the thin end of the wedge of a revolution that is needed in our attitude to the earth. Christians should be in the lead, and not on the defensive. Without "the salt" of the Gospel, this whole area of life could go badly wrong in just the way that St Paul saw many centuries ago.

111

12 GOOD AND EVIL

THE SEARCH FOR KNOWLEDGE

I often find people asking something like this: "But why are some people so fascinated by weird things such as *stoicheia*, speaking in tongues, witch-craft, prophecy, healing and all that? Why can they not be satisfied with ordinary down-to-earth Christianity?"

Or to look at the same question from another point of view, we may well wonder why in bookshops nowadays one will usually find a large selection of books on non-Christian religions, mysticism, occult themes and witch-craft, whereas the section on Christian literature is usually smaller and shows very little imagination.

The answer to both questions is made up of a number of factors, and no two people are alike, but for most of us it is a mixture of four elements:

(1) People who have been made to feel powerless and insignificant see the occult*, on the charismatic side or on the New Age side, as a way to get power and to "be somebody". We have already gone into the dangers of power-seeking and of ego-tripping, so we do not need to say any more about this.

---

*No doubt some of my Charismatic friends will be protesting at my referring to their "line" as occult (which means "secret"). Yet let me assure them that as far as ordinary church folk are concerned, and even more so as far as outsiders are concerned, tongues, prophecy, "knowledge" and healing are very occult!

---

(2) Some people have a deep gut-feeling that the materialistic view of life is not right and they want to get out of the closed system in which they have been brought up. They long for a glimpse of their true habitat. They feel, rightly, that they have been brought up on a *sub*-natural way of life, and they want to find that other dimension which is truly human, and which many people call *super*natural. This can lead them into that adventure which we call FAITH, heading out into the unknown like Abraham of old. It is a search for spiritual reality, for GOD. It can also lead to an unhealthy pre-occupation with anything "supernatural". Once more, we have dealt with that danger already, so we can leave it behind.

(3) There is the human thirst for KNOWLEDGE, that inquisitive drive which leads to new discoveries at every level. We shall look at that now.

(4) There is the basic human desire for some sort of GUIDANCE in dealing with the problems of life, realising that there is a point at which human help comes to an end. We must also look at that.

There is nothing wrong with the human search for knowledge in itself, but it can go very badly wrong.

CURIOSITY

It is natural that people find this world in which we live fascinating, and one of the reasons for the interest in the so-called "forbidden areas" is sheer curiosity, an aspect of our need to know and understand how things work. This curiosity is part of our make-up. Very early in life children develop an insatiable curiosity as to how and why things are what they are. Different people tend to be drawn to different areas of knowledge, and, naturally, some are more inquisitive than others.

People sometimes bring in "The Tree of the knowledge of good and evil" from Genesis 2 to suggest that it is our thirst for knowledge which leads to trouble, but this does not hold water, for there are different words for knowledge in most languages, and the word here is TO KNOW PERSONALLY, not TO KNOW ABOUT. The story in Genesis 2 has nothing to do with gaining more knowledge *about* God's world in order to be a responsible steward of it, as is commanded in Genesis 1:26; it *is* about our human desire to *experience* good and evil, so as to be in control of our own destiny as we saw earlier.

Certainly, authoritarian leaders in church or in state often resist the gaining of knowledge by their subjects, for radical new knowledge always makes one re-arrange one's whole thinking, and this is often uncomfortable for those who have a vested interest in things as they are. There is something very unhealthy about the sort of Christians who unthinkingly accept the comforts resulting from scientific research, including many electronic musical gadgets, but who at the same time suggest that further search for knowledge is wrong.

KNOWLEDGE AND SALVATION

Yet knowledge itself cannot save the individual or humanity as a whole. St Paul summed it up when he said, "And though I have the gift of prophecy, and understand all mysteries, and all knowledge... and have not love, I am nothing." That was a very important statement in his day, for there were people called GNOSTICS*, who, influenced by

Greek ideas, thought that it was by the imparting of secret knowledge that people grew spiritually. These Gnostics were infiltrating the churches, impressing people with esoteric (secret) knowledge, turning the church into yet another "mystery religion" such as those which were common in the Roman Empire. If they had succeeded, the church would have faded out along with the other mystery religions.

The Gospel is quite clear,then, that we are not saved by knowledge, but by GRACE (love-in-action). For instance many a person has responded to the Gospel story as a child, and has remained a Christian for life. Or again, many a simple soul, full of love for God and for people has had badly mistaken ideas about the world... perhaps thinking it flat. The vital, saving response of human love to the Divine Love requires very little knowledge, and conversely one may have much theological knowledge and very little love. At the basic level we have to "become little children", and the brainy have no advantage over the simple. If knowledge were the key to salvation, then the clever and the educated would have an unfair advantage. However, of course we gain knowledge as we grow, and we learn to love God with our MINDS... as Jesus taught (Mark 12:30).

* See William Barclay, *Study Guide on Colossians* for very interesting information about Gnostics.

THE PLACE OF KNOWLEDGE
Yet knowledge does have a place: when Pasteur and others of his time discovered germs and the need for sterilizing medical equipment, that was extra knowledge. Millions of wounded have survived who would once have died. Millions of mothers have survived childbirth who would once have died after it. Some of Pasteur's contemporaries said, "The issues of life and death are with God, this is tampering with God's prerogative". Yet today Christian doctors are no less careful about sterilizing their instruments than others! Knowledge about hygiene is certainly not "necessary for salvation", but it is important.

On the other hand we know only too well that when human knowledge is extended, it can be disastrous. The way we have used scientific knowledge is polluting the planet and threatening it with destruction. At the same time we must also face the fact that only properly conducted scientific research can give us the tools to correct the wrongs already done to earth. This double-edged weapon principle which we see with regard to scientific knowledge, surely applies to extending human knowledge in any field, including the psychic.

Inevitably there are those whose particular concern is to push the frontiers of knowledge forward in these areas of human exploration, including the psychic areas. Yet we must not be deceived into thinking that this is the way of salvation for individuals, for the race or for planet Earth. New knowledge in the psychic realm may be more dangerous than in more material places. That is not to say, however, that it is wrong to seek knowledge in these areas.

Rudolf Steiner said: **"For every one step you take in the pursuit of higher knowledge, take three in the perfection of your own character"**.

POWER

Knowledge always gives us power to manipulate both our environment and our fellow human-beings. We can, of course, enjoy the search for knowledge for itself, but, as the scientists whose work produced the atomic bomb discovered to their cost, one cannot divorce pure science from political power.

Of course most people who seek new knowledge, be it in science or in the psychic realms, think that they are doing so for good reasons, to help humanity. Yet we humans have a terrible capacity to deceive ourselves, and to think that our own motives are pure, even while we see how mixed are the motives of others! We thought of this when we looked at "healing". As the self-deception grows we become sure that we know what is best for others, and a terrible amount of damage is done in this world by people who have this certainty! The more knowledge they have the more dangerous they are. The way they manipulate people, and "liquidate" them too, "all for their own good", is more diabolic than the obvious "sins".

It all boils down to a simple fact: there is a difference between KNOWLEDGE and WISDOM. Very simple people can have a real wisdom, and people whose minds are loaded with information can be very foolish. As St Paul writes in 1 Corinthians 6: "Knowledge puffs up, love builds up". Indeed the whole Bible rates wisdom higher than knowledge, and our world today needs more wisdom rather than more knowledge, which keeps on arriving, relentlessly.

There are, then, two ways in which things can go wrong:
(1) The naive assumption that the acquisition of knowledge is always good in itself.

(2) The opposite assumption that seeking for knowledge is itself evil.

The obscurantists who take the second view will not have read this far, so we can forget them. Those who venture blithely forward assuming that all is well, ignore the warning of many old myths, such as the Faust story, that in the search for knowledge one meets what McNutt refers to as "the malevolent and intelligent force" which, regretfully, we conclude to be part of life's experience.

THE OCCULT

As we saw earlier, "occult" means hidden, and many things which we now take for granted would have been thought "occult" two centuries ago. As human knowledge of the wonderful, interlocking complexities of God's world grows, so things which were once occult become common knowledge.

Coming back to what we saw when we were thinking about dowsing for water, occult knowledge becomes evil when it is kept occult, hidden, in order to give the knower power over others. That which we have come to know must be shared for the common good, and then it is no longer occult. Of course not everybody can understand everything: for instance I still cannot understand how the TV works, even though people have tried to explain it!

It is sometimes asserted that there are areas of creation which human beings are forbidden to explore, forbidden areas. It is often suggested that the mysteries of genetics are such an area, and that knowledge of DNA etc should remain occult. Yet the Bible does not mark out any such borders marked "Forbidden". On the other hand, we tremble at the possibilities such research opens up for us unless we take a good many more than the three steps in spiritual growth which Steiner suggested!

In a number of New Age books we find assertions that Jesus gave occult teaching which the disciples did not hand on in the Gospels as we have them. Against this, we have His own sayings: "What I have told you in private, shout from the house-tops", "There is nothing hidden [occult] which shall not be revealed", and to Pilate, "I taught nothing in private but taught openly in the Temple". From the earliest days, this idea of secret teaching has allowed people to attribute all sorts of sayings to Jesus, which was why it became necessary to define what was authentic and what was not. The process continues today!

SOME CONCLUSIONS

* If a person's life is properly focused in love for God and love for others, then it is right to study, seeking more knowledge in one's own specific field at any level.

* New knowledge must be integrated into the pattern of fulfilling the purpose of God for one's life.

* We must take three steps in spiritual growth (i.e. in love for God and His Creation) for every one step in knowledge.

* We must seek wisdom first, then we will attract what knowledge we need, guided by the Holy Spirit.

In the self-centred life, knowledge serves the ego-trip, and there is a special temptation to regard knowledge about spiritual and psychic things as good in itself. Fascination with the supernatural is dangerous.

WHAT, THE DEVIL?

Having alluded to the "malevolent and intelligent force" which seems to be evident in the universe, and remembering what we mentioned when considering witchcraft, we must now take a serious look at this force. Those exploring the psychic would be well-advised to take some note of it, but it is an area of disagreement between New Agers and Charismatics.

As we have noted, some New Age people actually go in for Luciferic Initiation, and some rock music groups blatantly glorify Satan. However most New Age people in normal life play this down. Under oriental influence they tend to deny the actual existence of evil, and in reaction against a fear-laden Christian fundamentalism they also play down sin. So perhaps we should try to take a balanced look at the subject!

NAMING THE FORCE

Traditionally Christians call it THE DEVIL or SATAN. Noel O'Donoghue in his book about St Patrick, *Aristocracy of Soul* has a memorable passage about Satan, describing an experience which many of us would recognize:

Satan was seen as a mighty annihilating or destroying force whose naked presence was utterly terrifying to the human spirit. This contact brought a kind of living annihilation... the total absence of God and all the messengers of goodness and mercy. The very words "devil" and "Satan" tell us something in themselves. DEVIL has two roots, the first is in the Greek word *diabolos - dia bolos*, throw apart. This points to disintegration and confusion, whereas GOD is concerned to unify, to reconcile all things to Himself in Christ (Ephesians 1:10). The second, older root is in the Hindu word *deva*, which we usually translate "god". However the *devas* are not GOD as we mean that word, even by Hindu standards, for in their teaching the man who has attained enlightenment is above the *devas*.

The name SATAN has a root in the Persian religion of Zarathustra, and means the Accuser. In Scots law, the one who is responsible for conducting the prosecution is called the Procurator Fiscal; just so, it is Satan who accuses and destroys, and it is God who justifies and saves. The wonderful story of JOB in the Bible begins with a vivid picture of this, with Satan as an official in God's court, seeking permission to test Job.

In John 12:31 Jesus refers to "the Prince of this world", the Greek word being *archon*, a prince under the authority of the king... or we might say, the "*deva* of this world", the devil. In Ephesians 2:2 once more Satan is called an *archon*, who is at work in the "children of disobedience". Now a prince is not a king. For instance if the Prince of Wales tried to set up a separate kingdom for himself in Wales, in order to be king, there would be quite a constitutional crisis! That sort of political event happened quite often in Biblical times. It was natural for them to see a parallel, in that Jesus was re-asserting the Kingship of God in planet earth.

You will notice that all these illustrations make it quite clear that we are not in a "dualistic" setting, or to explain it differently, we do not find ourselves in the midst of a God *v.* Satan match. We have already referred to the letters to the churches at Ephesus and at Colosse, which state quite clearly that all authorities at any level are "created by and exist for Christ". It is not a question of a contest between equals, good against evil. GOD IS GOD, and we believe that the final issue has been decided! While God is still giving Himself time to win the hearts and minds of the human race, there is no doubt as to the outcome.

PERSONAL APPEARANCES

It is strange how *little* is said about the devil in the Bible, and what there is is mostly in the passing, so to speak. No explanation is given... it is just there. Apart from the Introduction to the book of Job, Satan only makes two personal appearances, to borrow a phrase from the theatre. The first is in the story of Adam and Eve in Genesis 2 (assuming that the the serpent is a Satan-figure), the other is in the account of Jesus' temptations in the desert (Matthew 4:1ff & Luke 4:1ff).

In neither story do we have the conventional picture of a devil, familiar to us from mediaeval pictures. In both it poses as a kindly, concerned being, more reasonable than God. The tempter seems to suggest that God would be unreasonable not to approve of Jesus using his power to feed himself after such a fast. It quotes the Bible and refers to the temple, both of them religious things, and implies that Jesus might be lacking faith if he hesitates to jump off the pinnacle of the temple. Finally there is the suggestion that of course you have to admit that it is really the devil who rules this world, and if you want power to do good, you will have to use its methods to gain power in the first place. Many good men have fallen for this temptation.

It is only in the book of Revelation, when the curtain is drawn back and we see behind the scenes, that we glimpse the hideous, destructive force for what it is: The Beast.

The Christian insight, then, is that the whole of this world, from the material to the spiritual is infected by the disruptive, distorting force, and that in Jesus, the Christ, the corrective force of com-munion (being-at-one-with, or at-one-ment) has been offered to us. The Kingdom of God has been re-asserted and we are to live under God's authority and love. This does not safeguard us from the probing attacks of the devil, as the history of the church shows, but it assures us of the final victory. To quote again from *Aristocracy of Soul*:

> There is here, nevertheless, a battle that has to be faced and faced most inescapably along the higher reaches of the upward journey. Yet the Prayer of Jesus takes account of this as we ask the Father not to lead us into [the depths of] temptation.

That is why the more our search for knowledge and power moves from the material end of the spectrum towards the spiritual, the more likely we are to encounter the *diabolos*. It is no chance that Jesus' spiritual experience in his baptism, is followed not by elation and euphoria, which is what one would expect, but by a grim struggle in which his

119

motives are probed to the depths. Therefore one trembles when beautiful, naive people begin to venture where angels fear to tread, with no real basic theology or discipline. Many of the areas we have referred to are liable to lead one to being open to evil under the guise of light.

THE DISTORTER

For us, day by day, Satan is likely to appear as being reasonable, kindly, and Christian. It is quite willing to offer short-term healing, while slipping in seeds which will sprout darkness later. John Richards in his book *But Deliver us from Evil*, warns us that the devil's main weapon is DISTORTION. Not a frontal attack to get us to do evil, but to take something true and good, and to distort it, so that it causes disruption. We noted that tendency when we were looking at the way Christians become diabolic in their reaction to witch-craft.

On a wider canvas also we speak from bitter experience, for we see the movement for Charismatic Renewal subject to distortion, and it is precisely because Renewal is an important move forward in the life of the church, that the devil seeks to distort it. And equally because the New Age movement is a real new chapter for humanity, the devil would distort it to be anti-Christian.

None of us should speak as if we were fool-proof!

The devil has two ways of deceiving us, the first is to give us such a ridiculous picture of itself that we dismiss it. The second is to make us think that there is no danger, and that good intentions are enough. Consider, for instance:

(1) *The Christian group or congregation which has become obsessed with exorcism*, seeing demons in every illness, sowing a lot of fear in suggestible people. It is doing the devil's work very nicely, for people write them off as cranks, and think that this is what Christianity leads to.

(2) *The liberal group which reacts against this and ignores the reality of evil*. It is making the dangerous mistake of underestimating the opposition. It is also operating in shady territory, even if it does not realize it. A watered down Gospel suits the Devil very well.

We can see from all this that it is because of the very nature of the *diabolos* that it is difficult to take up a balanced attitude, yet it is vital that we do, for much is at stake. Therefore whether we are charismatic, New Age, or just interested in this whole area, we have to be clear about the ground which we have covered, stating strongly again:

* God created everything, and God saw that it was good.

* **The whole of our world, seen and unseen, is somehow infected at every level.**

The desire for knowledge and power which leads us to explore God's creation and to harness its resources brings us into temptation, and if we succumb, we come under a very real force which is malevolent and intelligent. So our motives and fears must be continually subject to the discipline of the Gospel as we explore God's basically good world, whichever aspect of that world we are drawn to explore.

We have already said that in Jesus we have the answer to the devil, and indeed we have. Yet we see zealous Christians becoming distorted and unbalanced. There is a continual struggle, spiritual warfare, to check ourselves and our findings theologically, psychologically, morally and to guard our relationships. This means allowing other people to guide us as to whether or not we are growing in love for God and for others, developing the simplicity of a little child, holding to faith in Jesus as Son of God, made flesh, crucified and risen for us.

In terms of the two groups we began with, we can agree with the Charismatics that some of the New Age folk are on dangerous ground, but would ask them to be sure that distortion is not entering into their own midst. It is easy to see where the devil is at work in others. We can equally rejoice in the open-ness of the New Age folk, but suggest that as they pick up techniques, ideas and practices from religions all over the world, they also learn the lessons of our Christian heritage, understand the theological issues, and test any new thing by the Gospel.

THE PROOF OF THE PUDDING TEST

Let us now look further at how the Distorter gets at us, looking at where our new gifts, knowledge, powers, techniques etc are leading us.

For instance, we have seen groups of people who amass an amazing mixter-maxter of religious ideas: a little bit of Hinduism, a touch of Buddhism, a sprinkling of Red Indian, and some supposed

Celtic religion (not the head-hunting part!). Such a group can go in ever decreasing esoteric circles, and the Distorter has a hay-day with them. This is miles away from the Jesus who led his disciples out into the world, "eating and drinking with sinners", mixing with people from whom conventional religion had taught them to steer clear, for fear of becoming contaminated. Such esoteric groups avoid the real confrontation with human suffering and sin which is the Way of the Cross. Therefore we must watch to see in which direction our exploration is leading us.

Having said that about New Age type groups, one must be fair and add that the same applies to charismatic groups. They too can become so involved in their preoccupation with the Gifts of the Spirit, so caught up with the latest insights about spiritual warfare*, that they become closed circles, instead of open fountains through which the healing stream flows out into the world. They become desperate to get people into their groups, while raising the barriers ever higher between them and "the world". They become less and less like Jesus who **"looked with compassion on the crowds, for they were like sheep without a shepherd"** (Matthew 9:36). In fact they tend to condemn the crowd. The old Distorter has succeeded there too.

One could go on giving illustrations: Peace movements which are distorted into trouble-makers, evangelical movements distorted into big businesses, healing movements distorted into money-raising concerns, and so on.

So much for other people but:

What is the distortion to which you are liable?

To sum it up, then, we must come back to the Lord's prayer: "Lead us not into temptation but deliver us from the evil". Struggle is inevitable, and testing situations are necessary for our growth, we accept this, but we pray that we shall not be led into such temptations (testing) without (but) being delivered from the evil one.

---

* One reads in many Charismatic books about "The Kingdom of Satan" or the "Kingdom of Darkness". This is unscriptural. In Colossians "the power of darkness" is referred to, but the Greek word *exousia* used here refers to authority conveyed by someone higher (one modern translation refers to Satan's "gloomy Kingdom of darkness", but this is not accurate). Jesus does use the illustration of a kingdom divided against itself, but this is not admitting that Satan is king. There is no reference to a kingdom of Satan, except that Satan himself claims it in tempting Jesus, and that is a lie by the "father of lies". There is reference, as we have seen,

to authority, and by sin we can come under that authority, the authority of fear. But there is only one KINGDOM, that is God's, and Jesus has established it, dealing with "the prince of this world".

A theological quibble? Believing that the world is handed over to Satan and that everything outside one's own theological circle is in the Devil's power, results in religious paranoia.

13 GUIDANCE

DISCRIMINATION

Once we are aware of the "other side", we are led to look at St John's advice to "test the spirits to see if they are of God." (1 John 4:1). St John is particularly concerned in his letter to sort out the real from the counterfeit, because by the time he was writing, as an old man, somewhere about the year 90 AD, there were a lot of counterfeits.

In our day and age too there are counterfeits, some very plausible, on both the New Age and Charismatic sides. Let us therefore see what St John gives as a warning. But first here is a proposition to prepare the way for St John. It is this: **The further any relationship moves up the spectrum from the physical to the spiritual, the more important it is that there is spiritual one-ness.**

To take a fairly mundane example: as long as my local shop-keeper stocks the right goods and does not try to cheat me, his personal life does not concern me. However the window-cleaner who sees into my home and enters it, sets me another problem. I have to be surer of his character.

From that superficial example, let us move on to more challenging levels up the spiritual end of the spectrum. If I am in a setting in which an "altered state on consciousness" is involved, then I must be very careful in whose company I am. (You will remember that an ASC is basically a state of consciousness in which my normal critical faculties are no longer guarding access to my inner being, to my psyche.)

To some extent this happens if two people have sex, or get drunk together, for in both cases the barriers between them are lowered, and feelings arise from the depths of which normally they may not be aware. This may lead to great happiness but only too often it leads to violence. Hence St Paul's warning about having sex with a prostitute*, for such a relationship is not just physical. Inevitably something psychic flows between those concerned.

---

* 1 Corinthians 6:15 "Fornication" means involvement with prostitutes. The word has the same root as pornography, with the suggestion of commerce. In New Testament times it was usually associated with the worship of other gods, with the prostitutes based on the heathen temples. The term used to be applied (wrongly) to any pre-marital sex.

In the same way one may safely talk about religion with anybody, or even go to services at a purely intellectual level, without "opening up" at all. However there comes a point at which there is a real opening of the psyche to the other. We know that "something has flowed". We come away from the relationship or from the service, knowing that something which goes beyond sound-waves has affected us, and we feel a lot better... or worse!

WORSHIP TOGETHER

We know a slightly deeper level of such opening up to each other when we join in singing together. As we saw earlier, the hypnotic repeating of choruses in a charismatic setting, the intoning of chants in other settings, and the performance of ritual are all ways in which the critical faculty is lulled, and people are made more suggestible. The drumming music of the disco, the stirring strains of martial music and many other such things, help to create a common mind, with the barriers between people lowered. Something then flows between people, as Hitler knew well in his Nuremberg rallies. In this way he got them to accept ideas which individually they would have rejected.

There was wisdom in the arrangement found in the early church: the first part of the service was open, and all were welcome, with teaching being the emphasis. Only when the catechumens (those under instruction) and seekers had left did the congregation go on to celebrate the Lord's Supper. They did not want anybody present who might disrupt the flow of the Spirit.

This points us to the fact that while we may talk, discuss and play sports with anybody, we have to be careful and discriminating about the company in which we undertake any self-opening as referred to above, not least deep worship.

MEDITATION

This applies especially when we move on to an even deeper form of ASC: meditation, christian and non-christian. [Sometimes the word "meditation" is used simply for a time of reflection, and "contemplation" for the deeper state.] The aim of meditation is to cease from analytical, intellectual thought, and to be open to whatever one conceives as the object of life. "Be still and know that I am God"... "Let go and let God!"... such thoughts focus the Christian's meditation, while others have mantras etc.

If people meditate together, there is a really deep flow between them. We therefore have to choose carefully with whom we meditate .

TOUCHING

In some forms of massage, or in situations when people hold hands, or touch when sharing a deep emotion such as sorrow, or in the laying-on of hands, there is also a deep flow between those concerned. This is in fact the basis for a lot of "natural" healing, and we have all had *some* experience of it. However on several occasions we have had to help people who had a "natural gift of healing", and who had laid hands on a person from whom the negative discharge was stronger than the positive discharge from the healer, and the result was darkness in the one who had tried to heal. So once again we sound a note of caution to those who feel like dashing into laying hands on people for healing, or who go to "healers" for the laying on of hands.

An interesting insight into touching came to me recently: a qualified nurse working in a Rudolf Steiner clinic had been doing massage for patients. However when they found that she was pregnant they immediately stopped her doing so, because the baby within her needed all her natural energies, and it would be wrong to disperse them to patients. This underlines the fact that there is a real "flow" in these forms of touching. We have to be discriminating with regard to touching and being touched.

LIKE ATTRACTS LIKE

We have already noted that the law "like attracts like" operates as one moves into the deeper levels. This means that when we open ourselves up in these ways, we will tend to attract to ourselves the psychic forces in the environment or in the other person which echo our own deep feelings... feelings which we often hide in our normal state of consciousness. We may, with our conscious minds, mean to contact light and goodness, but once we surrender that control and allow the deeper self to surface, it is sometimes the darker, hidden urges which surface. Hence the guidance given by most spiritual directors, that such processes should not be done without proper supervision.

THE TESTS

How can we venture safely into this territory? St John gives us some tests: "Every spirit which confesses that Jesus, the Christ, is come in the flesh is of God" (1 John 4:1). In verse 15: "Whoever confesses that Jesus is Son of God, dwells in Him". In St John's day that was straightforward, but centuries of criss-crossing doctrines have made it hard for us. To illustrate this: for the Jews the father-son relationship was the best example of one-ness, whereas for us fathers and sons are very separate people!

SON OF GOD

Therefore when THEY said that Jesus was Son of God, they were stressing his ONEness with the Father, whereas WE tend to think it means two separate people. For them it meant that to see Jesus was to know what the Father is like... "He that hath see me hath seen the Father", said Jesus (John 14:9). He said this not as a boast, but to re-assure them that there was nothing to fear.

This means that if a person says that Jesus is "one of the great spiritual masters", on the level with the Buddha, Mahomet and so on, he is undoing the Gospel, even if it sounds like superior wisdom. Either God has Himself entered the world in human form to reconcile us to Himself or He has not. We may honour the great spiritual teachers, and many of us would rate the Buddha very highly indeed, but he, for instance, would have been horrified at the idea of being regarded as a god... in fact he refused to speculate about God. Either Jesus IS "The Word made flesh", the self-expression of God, or he is not. Mahomet only claimed to be a prophet, and the other great spiritual leaders all pointed away from themselves. St John's warning, then, is to beware of any teaching which undermines that one-ness with the Father.* We may discuss with people who disagree with us about who Jesus is, but we should not enter into meditation or deep prayer with them.

* See *Return to the Centre*, Bede Griffiths. With his experience of eastern religion he traces out the difference between Jesus and the other great religious figures.

SON OF MAN

On the other hand St John warns us to beware of what undermines the "offensive" humanity of Jesus. Paul refers to the Cross as a stumbling-block, an offence... foolishness. So-called wisdom, in his day and in ours, tries to lessen this offence and to make it more acceptable to "decent, educated people". The idea of a man being tortured to death, saying, "he that hath seen me hath seen the Father", seems ludicrous. Yet any teaching which sounds "wise" and which tries to get away from the offence of looking at the crucified carpenter and saying: "Behold your God", is false. One rather sophisticated group of spiritually minded people spoke of worshipping "the dis-crucified Christ", and others make much ado of the "Cosmic Christ", but avoid the crunch of that MAN being executed painfully for our sins. Such sentiments may sound sophisticated and broad-minded, but they undo the Gospel, and play right into the Distorter's hands.

LOVE

St John's other test, right through that Letter, is simply LOVE. The Devil likes religious people, they do so much harm. The more religious they are the more they play into its hands *if they are not loving*. And by LOVE we mean the costly self-giving which we see in Jesus. One can find "new spirituality" Christians so caught up in their esoteric discoveries that they never get their hands dirty in the places where human beings suffer and are degraded. One can find ardent "baptized in the Spirit" Christians who live in their own wealthy social environment, unaware of the Way of the Cross, but often very powerful in a worldly sense. And one can also find zealous and doctrinally correct Christians, utterly lacking in love.

In all these cases, the cosy feeling of an in-group is mistaken for the Love of Christ, whose hall-mark is an outpouring of self for the world.

St John, then, gives us these three pointers, by which we can find our way. If we do have visions, or visitors, earthly or angelic, claiming to be from God, we must test them:

* What do they say about Jesus? Do they confess him to be truly Son of God and truly Son of Man, crucified and risen? Any dodging that issue will indicate that the Distorter is at work.

* Are they are showing a Christ-like love?

If we have an angelic or "spirit" visitor, we should apply this test before listening to any message which purports to come from God.* If they are truly from God they will expect us to obey the biblical injunction to check them out, and will not be offended.

* As a note on the above, I would report that I once read much spiritualist literature, both the Psychic News and various books which claimed to have revelations from "beyond", in order to see what was said of Jesus, applying St John's test. I found that the "revelations" were as varied from "the other side" as they are from ours! Some were atheist, and had no place for Jesus. Some had him as a Great Master, and some came near to an orthodox position.

When one looked at the morality they were suggesting, it was very bland and acceptable to middle-class people, with little of "the turning the world upside down" ethic that is typical of Jesus.

I also noted that, for instance, some asserted that reincarnation is the explanation of life's mysteries, while others asserted that we progressed to different planes beyond, and did not come back to earth. It seemed that there were contradictory teachings "over there" just as there are here, and that therefore one could not assume that that which came from beyond was necessarily nearer the truth than what we find here.

These communications were maybe indeed from "the other side", but they failed St John's tests, and that was enough for me! I found much deeper insights in my contemporaries.

If we are choosing a minister, priest, spiritual counsellor or religious leader, we must also apply these tests. We may listen to interesting ideas from many sources, but we must be very discriminating about whom we allow to influence us at a deep level, for instance by leading our worship.

It would be wise to learn from the experience of St Martin, one of the greatest of saints. One day while he was praying, a glorious Christ-figure stood before him saying: "Martin, worship me". Martin immediately said, "Show me Your Wounds", and the figure disappeared, with a glimpse of cloven hooves under the glorious robe.

We must be discriminating too about those with whom we meditate or pray at depth. We might be friendly, and have interesting discussions with many varied folk, but we would need to be very guarded about taking part in their worship or meditation. In fact on several occasions, when a person who was genuinely filled by the Holy Spirit joined such a group, the group found it so disturbing that they asked the Christian to leave: he/she was "disturbing the spirits".

We may also be discriminating about whom we ask to pray for us: I remember one occasion when a very spiritually sensitive person was sharing a problem with a group, and when it came to prayer she said firmly and lovingly: "I'm sorry, but I don't want that person praying for me". It turned out that the person indicated had had spiritualist connections. This may also account for the strange fact that one of the great teachers in this area, Agnes Sanford, said that she found there was always trouble if she prayed for people who were spiritualist. It was like mixing AC and DC current in electricity, she said.

On the other hand, if we follow Jesus, we shall be very undiscriminating about our acquaintances and friends, even shockingly so, as he was! Yet he did not invite the crowd up the Mount of Transfiguration or into the Garden of Gethesemane. He was discriminating as to whom he invited to share these experiences, and we too must be discriminating as to whom we undertake any activity in which the barriers go down and our inner being lies open.

DISCERNMENT

Several times already in this book we have referred to the Gift of Discernment, so let us tackle the subject in more detail now. It is important because it is mostly by what they claim to be discernment that Charismatics pronounce various New Age activities to be evil.

We use this word to describe the Gift of the Holy Spirit which enables us to discern good and evil in situations and in people. People with this gift "see" darkness or light, and are able to guide the healing process accordingly. At a very low level many of us are often able to discern whether a person has been involved with spiritualism. On the other side we are often able to know if a person has really been "born again of the Spirit", or whether in fact, in spite of shouting the odds about being a "born again Christian" s/he is actually living on artificial religious emotion.

This Gift is of especial value when dealing with people who "hear voices". It is almost impossible to tell from ordinary observation whether they are actually mentally ill or whether they are, as they often think, oppressed by demonic elements or by the voices of the dead. It also helps to decide whether a person is DEpressed and needing counsellng and perhaps medication, or whether he/she is OPpressed and needing prayer for deliverance.

Therefore one would think that this would be an important gift in sorting out the issues at which we have been looking. In many ways it is, and we should certainly pray for discernment in these areas. However, knowledge gained this way is "non-transferable", like British Rail tickets. For example we invited a Christian Homoeopathic practitioner to speak at a conference, only to be told that the practitioner's pastor had been given discernment that homoeopathy was of the devil and as the result thousands of pounds worth of books and medicines had been burned.

Our own prayer and discernment had pointed us to *some* evil, but not to the whole system as being evil. (It is possible that we might have had negative results on some modern medical practices!) From this we see that while in any one group, a discernment may be accepted because the person who gave it is known to be reliable, those outside may not be convinced. On the other hand when two packets of homoeopathic medicine came through the post for us, I phoned a person with discernment and said: "I've two things here I'd like you to pray about." (I was careful not to give any indication as to what they were). As I held the first, she said, "I don't know what it is, but I'm running my hands through my hair saying, 'Don't make me touch it'". Then I held the other remedy, and she said: "That's not so bad." She was taken aback when I told her what it was that I had been holding, because she was sympathetic to homoeopathy.

Such an experience cannot be brushed aside lightly, yet one cannot make sweeping conclusions on the strength of it. As we saw earlier, we are here to learn to make responsible decisions, and we must not look for short-cuts. It convinces no reasonable person to say that one has discerned evil in some practice. It may serve as a warning light, but that is all. As we saw in previous sections of this book, practices which are harmless parts of God's creation by nature, can be affected by evil, and what is discerned as evil may not be the practice itself but the way in which it is being used. On the other hand something which might be a perfectly valid form of activity for some people, might be a serious distraction from the Lord's work for another. For instance a group which was being called to be prayerful, and to exercise a deeply spiritual ministry, might be distracted from this by people joining it who wanted to practise herbalism, reflexology, and such-like, whereas these people might well enrich another community.

IN PRACTICE

What if after a time of prayer, a Christian Group discerns something evil in some practice, or in some person? We have given some examples above.

The worst thing one can do, as a general rule, is to take the head-on approach. Telling people that they, or their approach is evil, just arouses fear, and fear is a false ally. The first thing is to learn that there is a profound difference between:

131

A   The person from a non-Christian background who is finding his/ her way towards God through unorthodox channels, but who is really searching for the Truth.

and

B   The person, perhaps with a Christian background, who is looking for short-cuts, for more exciting ego-trips, or even for power.

Type A may well have tried some approaches which have left a taint of evil, but if the life of the Christian Community is truly loving and light-filled, either the person concerned will become aware of the need for cleansing, or else the evil will just wither away. Such a person must know first that they are accepted and loved in the community before being faced with the fact of being in some way "unclean". Naturally the people who have discerned the evil will take the authority of Jesus and bind it, without the person knowing, until it is the right time for it to be dealt with. Terrible damage can be done by exhibitionistic people who revel in "power" and who take every opportunity to pounce on some poor victim... ostensibly for their own good and for the glory of the Gospel.

Type B is a very different kettle of fish! Here there must be real repentance as the person faces the true motives involved. Then must follow the renunciation of whatever it is which has gone wrong. We have referred earlier to several people who had to do this after recourse to use of the pendulum. Since such a person can poison and mislead any group, one has to take a strong line.

To sum this up, then: both New Age and Charismatic Christians move into areas in which they are open to psychic forces which may be good or bad, remembering that the most evil ones always appear as angels of light! In this area we very much need the gift of discernment.*

* There is a satanic version of discernment, as we found when we were struggling to free somebody from a coven. It became necessary for this person to visit the house in which the coven met, and, realizing that there was real danger, we suggested rallying a number of Christians who were unknown in the town, to stand around in the street, ready for emergencies. "That would be no use," the patient said, "*they* can see the light round Christians and would realize that something was afoot with all those Christians in the street at once." So we discovered that those in witch-craft can discern Christians.

As with all Gifts of the Spirit, we must cross-check, to make sure the Distorter is not at work, and while discernment is a good indicator, it must always be accompanied by Bible Study and responsible thought. We must never try to force on others that which has come to us from discernment. We may say: "This is what has come to us through prayer and discernment, but we hope that you will check it for yourself."

HOW DOES GOD GUIDE US?

Many of the areas we have looked at are concerned with the human need for guidance in solving some problem. When we were little children we looked to our parents, thinking that they knew all the answers and could guide us. When we become the parents we find that there are still problems before us in which we need to look to "someone" higher.

It is this feeling that there MUST be some Great Parent which leads us to the sort of exploring which has been the subject of much of this book. There is one sense in which this is a right feeling, but it can lead people into the abrogation of reponsibility and into a sort of dependency or bondage to "someone" who claims to be able to give this sort of guidance. We have seen repeatedly that we are meant to be living as responsible children of God, learning to make decisions and to be open to God's guidance. It is therefore time that we looked in more detail at what is meant by "God's guidance".

Before we do so let us sharpen up the question:
How does God guide the mechanic at his workbench, the manager making up his mind about redundancies, the doctor facing a difficult patient, the computer operator puzzling over a problem? In these, as in most important decisions we make, we do not have time or the opportunity to refer to the prayer of a group, or to seek out a true prophet!

Then there are the political problems:
How does God guide the people of Scotland about their future relationship with England, as well as the many down-to-earth problems facing Britain and the rest of Europe... let alone the future of the earth!

Too many books and articles on guidance seem to suggest that the choices are in the realm of decisions about the life of the Christian church or group. Yet where they really count is in the day by day life of ordinary people. This came up earlier when we wondered about dowsing and pendulums.

CHILDREN, NOT ROBOTS

Jesus said to the first twelve disciples: "I do not call you servants, for a servant does not know what his master does. I call you friends...". We are not meant to be robots waiting around to be told what to do, with no minds of our own. That was the mistake of the elder brother in the Parable of the Prodigal Son in Luke 15 (it should be called the Story of the Forgiving Father): he did what he was told, and that was that. The father said: "Son, you are always here with me, and everything I have is yours." In other words, he could have had a party with his friends any time! That brother was wrong in waiting around hoping to be told that he could have a party, when he should have gone ahead and had one!

In the same way there is a wrong sort of "seeking guidance" even from God - a failure to use the understanding he has already given us. Here, in contrast, are some of the ways in which we can be guided as children of God:

INNER RENEWAL BY THE HOLY SPIRIT

This is beautifully set out in Romans 12. St Paul says that real worship is when we offer our bodies as living sacrifices to God. This means that in the light of the Love which God has shown us, we offer, not animals which we have killed, but our living bodies, putting them at God's disposal so that His love may be expressed through us. As the old Gaelic prayer puts it:

> O Christ, Thou Son of God,
> Thou one eternal Word,
> Be Thou made flesh in me
> Do Thou Thy Will in me.

This loving response to God's Love opens us up, so that we can be inwardly renewed by His Spirit, instead of being moulded by the environment and by society. Renewed in this way by the Love of God we come to know what God wants done, which is what is meant by the phrase "the Will of God", and St Paul describes it as "the lovely Will of God", for the Greek word *kalos* refers to goodness in an artistic sense rather than in a moral sense. A hymn puts it neatly:

> Breathe on me Breath of God,
> Fill me with life anew,
> That I may love what Thou dost love,
> And do what Thou wouldst do.

In this way we grow into being the children of God who act in harmony with the Father as we care for each other and for His Creation. Of course we make mistakes, but **it is more important that we should *learn* through making mistakes than that we should get it "all right" without having learned decision-making.** Any teacher knows that with sufficient prompting, all her children could get all the right answers. Yet that is not the way in which we learn for ourselves.

THROUGH THE BIBLE

Let me share my own experience. During the war I was in a military hospital, not expecting to live. It seemed the right thing to do to ask for a Bible, and the chaplain duly brought me one. In spite of my desperate spiritual need, I could make nothing of it. That surprised me, for twice in situations of deep need I had opened a Bible and found help. We have to be careful, then, not to be too glib about getting guidance from the Bible.

Admittedly many others have had my earlier experience of opening the Bible at random and finding help, yet this can slip down into superstition. It is through regular, disciplined study in a fellowship of others walking in the same direction through life, that it "comes alive" and our characters are re-shaped. As we commented earlier, God seems to use the random means mainly for beginners.

In disciplined study of the Bible we learn and grow, but it is surprising how often a verse will suddenly "come alive" and one knows that "this means you". For this "coming alive" three things are usually needed:

* The printed book, preferably in language we understand easily;

* The fellowship of those in whom the Spirit is at work, re-creating and guiding;

* **An honest facing of the real situations of everyday life.**

Those who have only heard the Bible read in church on Sunday have missed out badly, for the Bible was written for small groups under pressure, and that is where it "speaks" most clearly.

Of course we all know that "you can prove anything out of the Bible", and "the devil can quote scripture". Too often Christians have made fools of themselves and have brought disrepute on the Gospel by arguing about verses lifted out of their context and twisted to support one side against the other.

135

It is only too easy to confuse two things:

(1) The joy when a passage "lights up" and we know that God's Word is speaking to us.

(2) The elation in finding a verse which backs up what we think.

Perhaps the classic example of such a mistake happened at Dunbar, when the Scots army was in a strong postion, while Oliver Cromwell and his troops were exhausted and in no condition to attack such a stronghold. However the Scots ministers had a prayer meeting and concluded that some verses quoting what the Lord had said to King David in 1000 BC applied to the Scots army then and there. They persuaded the generals, against all their thinking, to sweep down on the English "for the Lord had delivered them into our hands". Cromwell could hardly believe his eyes when he saw what was happening, and made short work of the Scots army. The misuse of Scripture can be dangerous!

Another mistake is to think that the Bible can provide a proof text to show the right thing to do in every situation. This is very much how the Pharisees saw it, and how Moslems see the Koran. The result of this view is that those who hold it have to develop a whole complex of rules and regulations to cover every situation in life. There was a time when the Roman Catholic Church tried this, and the result is amusingly summed up in Lodge's novel, *How far can you go?*

As an example of finding nothing directly in the Bible to guide us, I would refer to a situation brought before me by some medical friends. The kidney machine was fully booked, when a brilliant student developed kidney trouble and was going to need regular dialysis. This put the doctors in the position of having to decide: should they tell an old man who had been on it for years: "Don't come back", and let him die? Or should they say to the student: "Sorry, no room"? By the time a new machine was built, the student would be dead.

There was no one Bible verse to solve their problem. They had to choose between the two lives, and having made the choice, act as kindly as possible, trusting to the mercy of God. To have carried a burden of guilt, once the choice had been made, would have made them unhealthy, and less effective as doctors. Only a deep understanding of the grace of God, and a trust in His redeeming power to cope with human shortcomings could meet their need.

Incidentally, if the old man had been me, I hope that I would have had the grace to say: "I'll come off, let the lad have my place." But I would have said also: "I do not want the grisly business of death by

kidney failure. Please help me to die with dignity and a clear mind."
Now would that have been suicide and euthanasia? There is a question
for guidance!

It is very noticeable that Jesus did not leave us a code of conduct,
nor even a list of rituals to be performed, but continually referred us
back to the very nature of God. In the Sermon on the Mount we have
a number of quite separate insights into what life in the Kingdom of God
is like, but in each instance Jesus refers us back to the very nature of
God, so that we, in seeking guidance for any other situation, have to
make our own pilgrimage into the Holy Place. Above all we have to
make the life of Jesus our bread and butter... "The Bread of Life", and
as we do so our decisions will be more in line with his purposes.

GUIDANCE FOR SPECIAL OCCASIONS
There are however means of guidance for special occasions.

PROPHECY
There are times when God speaks directly to His Church
through a prophet, which means "a spokesman" (foretelling the future
is not necessarily part of prophecy). St Paul in 1 Corinthians 14 rates
this very highly as a Gift of the Holy Spirit. Yet still prophecies have
to be checked over, for even the greatest saints can get off beam at
times! A true prophecy must ring true to the Gospel, and it will usually
have some element in it which could not have been invented by the
human agent. That is where foretelling the future sometimes comes in.

Therefore when God wants something done which could not be
worked out by human reasoning, He may use a prophet to make His will
known. Of course, in the every-day examples at the start of this chapter,
one could hardly take time off work to consult a prophet! Let us also
note, however, that becoming dependent on somebody with a gift of
prophecy is wrong.

DREAMS AND VISIONS
The best example is the one we quoted earlier, when Peter was
in trance on the rooftop, and had the vision of a sheet let down from
heaven with all sorts of beasts in it. The vision was given because he was
being asked to do something which went against all his religious
upbringing: to go into the house of a Roman officer. After Peter's
experience at Pentecost, he should have known better, and have been

137

free from his Jewish inhibitions, but God was merciful and gave him a vision.

The "scenery" in the vision came from Peter's own mind. On rooftops people often erected a sunshade so that they could sit under it in the breeze. There may or may or not have been such a sheet stretched over Peter, but there certainly would have been on some neighbouring houses. The strange "catch" would come from his days as a fisherman. So the Spirit uses images in Peter's mind to express a spiritual truth. In all visions and dreams we have to be careful to sift out what is the message from God and what is the scenery drawn from limited human minds. (This is what people often fail to do when they read the Book of Revelation in the Bible. It is the greatest vision of all.)

Dreams and visions are not the normal way in which we are guided, but because of our weakness, God does use them occasionally. They are NOT a sign of spiritual superiority! If anything they are a sign of weakness. Normally we should not need them.

THE UNEXPECTED

God often works through very surprising means: a chance word overheard, a phrase in a book we are reading, a sermon in church... one could go on and on! The Swiss psychiatrist Paul Tournier commented that God often speaks to us through our wives, which is most inconvenient. Most men would far rather He spoke direct!

As we said earlier, God may speak to us through any part of His Creation, but we must not stipulate how He must do it in any one case. However, there are time when one just KNOWS: "That's it!"

THROUGH THE FELLOWSHIP OF THE HOLY SPIRIT

God does guide us often, through our worship together, through our study together, through our private prayer and study as well as through the other means we have outlined above when necessary. Often a sermon or a reading will be labelled: "This means you" - yet never in a way that frees us from responsible decision-making. Often too, the very act of sharing a problem brings us light.

LOOKING BACK

Often it is only when we look back on life that we see how in fact He has led us, even when we were quite unaware of it.

The best example of this is recorded in St John's Gospel chapter 14. The scene is the Last Supper: a sorely puzzled Thomas says, "We do not know where you are going so how can we know the way?" Poor man, he was needing a bit of guidance! Jesus' answer was, "I am the true and living way" (often put: I am the Way, the truth and the life). In other words, "You know ME. That is the way". It is in loving communion with HIM that we are guided safely through our work on earth and brought Home at last.

Often it is when God seems to be absent, and we feel defeated, as Thomas must have felt when they fled from the Garden of Gethsemane, that we find in fact that we were being guided and protected all the time. That is the deepest form of spirituality, not the apparently more exciting way of getting immediate guidance for everything.

14 QUESTIONS OF TIME
AND ETERNITY

REINCARNATION

Now we need to take a closer look at this belief which is very common among New Age people, but has been labelled as a heresy since very early in the history of the church.

First: **WHY SHOULD ANYBODY BELIEVE IN REINCARNATION?**

There are three main reasons:

1 EXPERIENCE

Many of us when visiting some place have the feeling of "I've been here before", when we know that we have not... not in this life anyway!.

I remember a lady in my parish in Edinburgh who took her daughter and grand-daughter across to Fife, to visit the Pittencrieff Glen. As they approached the gates, the grand-daughter, just a toddler, started talking happily about what was in this public park as if she knew it well. Once in, she knew her way round to where all the different attractions were to be found. Since she was much too young to be able to read, the only conclusion her puzzled mother and grandmother could come to was: "She's been here before, but not in this life."

A number of children have been recorded as having this sort of experience, and can even give the names of previous parents, which prove to be correct in many details. The strange thing is that by the time they are of school age, the memory has quite faded, and even if reminded of it they are quite blank.

A more serious example which has come my way is a lady who is sure that she is the reincarnation of a certain rather tragic figure in history, and that she has to make good the trouble she thinks that she caused centuries ago. This has dominated her whole life, so that she carries an intolerable burden, feeling that she has to do something which she is not in a position to do. Strangely she has produced several bits of evidence to back up her belief.

There are a number of books which go into great detail about such experiences and this gives rise to much discussion as to whether there is not a psychological explanation rather than a reincarnational one. The result is usually that those who want to believe the experience find that it is proved while those who do not want to believe it find it disproved! Back to Square One!

2 CONVENIENCE?

Reincarnation is a very comfortable belief if you are wealthy and healthy! If you believe that your *karma*, your life pattern is set strictly on a reward and punishment basis, then if you are wealthy and healthy it is because you have earned it. Those who are poor and unhealthy are in this condition as a punishment. Therefore while you may add to your good marks by giving alms, you would not do anything radical to change their condition. Where this belief is strong, as in the east, you do not find many social revolutions: a very handy belief for the upper classes!

3 ANSWERS

Reincarnation seems to explain some aspects of life that we find puzzling. For instance: how is it that some of us seem to have known and loved Jesus from our earliest days, even though we did not come from "Christian" homes? I think of one lady who was brought up in a strongly marxist atheist home, yet who loved Jesus from as long as she could remember, in spite of everything her parents could do to dissuade her. One could say that it was just childish cussedness, but it is strange.

The Camphill communities are based on the teaching of Rudolf Steiner. His teaching on the subject gives Jesus Christ and the Cross a central place in the whole process, and is quite different from the more usual oriental model. His teaching on reincarnation is closer to the Christian point of view, though still not orthodox.

On the basis of his understanding, Downs Syndrome people (mongoloid) receive special treatment; they are regarded as souls near the top of the reincarnational scheme, but who have over-intellectualised in a previous life, and now need to learn just to enjoy love and beauty. Hence the Camphill communities do a wonderful work with these people. Even those who disagree with their theory have to admire their practice, and some of those who are strongly orthodox in their Christian beliefs are put to shame by the loving care given in these communities.

These, then, are some of the reasons why people believe in reincarnation, while others would say that it is a devilish deception to hide from people the need to make up one's mind about the Gospel NOW.

Now another question: **IS REINCARNATION IN THE BIBLE?**

At first sight NO. However, if one looks more carefully, there are two references to the belief:

(1) The first is the case recorded in St John's Gospel chapter 9. The disciples see a man blind from birth begging at the roadside. They discuss the "WHY?" question, assuming that it must be a punishment. They ask Jesus whether it was that this man had sinned, or whether it had been his parents who had sinned. Now since he had been BORN blind, the obvious conclusion is that they were asking whether he had sinned in a previous life and had thus deserved this punishment. Some Biblical scholars try to get away from this obvious meaning by saying that rabbis believed that one could sin in the womb... it seems a bit far-fetched!

Jesus just swept the whole reward-and-punishment element aside: "It is not that this man sinned, or his parents", he said. "However, in order that the works of God may be seen in him, I must get on with the work I have been given to do while I have the chance"... and then he healed him.*

So, in this case the idea of *karma* is discounted by Jesus.

(2) On the other hand, it seems clear that Jesus saw John the Baptist as the reincarnation of Elijah (see Matthew 11:14, 17:11-12, Mark 9:11-13). Scholars disagree, however, as to whether this is a literal view of reincarnation, or whether he is speaking figuratively (as when we say, "So-and-so is a chip off the old block").

Sometimes the saying, "What a man sows, he shall reap" is quoted as biblical support for the idea; recently a famous person on TV attributed it to Jesus, claiming that he said it in terms of reincarnation. It was, of course, St Paul who quoted the proverb (i) in support of generous giving in 2 Corinthians 9:6, and (ii) as a warning against habits which become addictions in Galatians 6:7.

We can conclude that the idea was in the background (and we know this also from sources outwith the Bible), but it faded into insignificance beside the glory of the Gospel: the Kingdom of God is in your midst NOW.

---

*I have paraphrased the Lord's answer, trying to keep to the Greek words, but re-arranging the punctuation, taking this liberty because there was no punctuation in the original.

Finally we ask: **WHAT IS AGAINST BELIEVING IN REINCARNATION?**

The first thing is the belief: **"When anyone is in Christ there is a new creation"** (2 Cor 5:17). When a person turns to God in Christ, then the old order is done away with, and we start afresh. There is no point in digging into supposed past lives. From that point one's future is worked out in collaboration with our Heavenly Father, not with an impersonal *karma*. Admittedly our Father has His own purposes for our lives, but this is very different from the oriental concept of *karma*.

Another point against the idea is the verse Hebrews 9:27: **"It is our human lot to die once, with judgement to follow"** (REB) and that seems clear enough, although the point is being made about there being no need for repeated sacrifices, not repeated lives. Those who believe in reincarnation take the verse to mean that there is a point to which the soul comes in its journey when it confronts the Gospel and *then* it must accept or reject the Love of God in Christ. On this occasion the process stops and is summed up.

This, of course, begs a large question: When does a person get a fair chance to hear the Gospel? One finds so often that people who have been brought up in narrow-minded, judgmental families turn against the faith and who would blame them? Others have only seen Christianity as dull respectability with boring services. If that is all they know, who would blame them for ignoring it? However, we can surely leave to Jesus such questions, after all he suffered at the hands of the ultra-religious, and he knows it from the inside!

TORAH AND KARMA

When one looks carefully, there is a strong similarity between our attitude to reincarnation and our attitude to what St Paul refers to, especially in Galatians, as "the law" (*torah*): the moral law and ritual commandments of the Old Testament. The reward-and-punishment teaching seems strong in both the Old Testament and in oriental karmic teaching.

Both tend to suggest that you somehow climb nearer to God by earning marks for good behaviour, and drop down the scale if you do wrong. Both forms of teaching lead us to be preoccupied with escaping:

(a) the oriental seeks deliverance from this awful cycle of birth, suffering, death, which seems to go on and on.

(b) St Paul cries out with regard to "the law": "Who shall deliver me from the body of this death?" He traces how "the law", meant to be our teacher to lead us to Christ, becomes a bondage and a prison from which we need deliverance. He is quite incredulous when the Galatians, our ancient Celtic cousins, like so many of our present day ones, seem caught up again in bondage to the law when they had tasted the freedom which is in Christ: "O foolish Galatians, who has bewitched you?".

Whether we come from the background of concern for the moral law and strict religious observance in the Pharisaic pattern, or whether we come from the background of working our way painfully up the karmic scale, the good news is that it is by Grace, by the free Love of God that we can move from wherever we are spiritually right into Communion with the Father through Jesus, and know the Power of the Spirit in our lives.

It is essential for all of us to make this shift of attitude, for after all, one does not need to read heavy books on psychology to know that love cannot be earned. For instance if children are trying to *earn* the love of their parents, then something is badly wrong. They may be "good children", but the goodness is phoney, and the "goodness" of adults who are concerned to earn merit is phoney too!

You cannot earn the Love of God, for God loves you already.

It is through love freely offered that we are put right, not by "works of the law" nor by working out our *karma*. To turn down the offer of a free, loving relationship with God, and to insist on working out one's own "thing" be it in terms of the moral law or of of *karma*, is folly, as Paul saw when dealing with the Galatians. What was meant to be a "schoolmaster to bring us to Christ" then becomes an evil bondage. It is a subtle form of spiritual pride if we insist on working our own passage when we are offered a loving relationship!

The healthy attitude is to leave the past, however we conceive it, in the Mercy of God, and get on with working out the future with God as His fellow-workers. The Lamb of God takes upon himself the sins and mistakes of the past so that we may be free to start afresh... be born again as new people here and now, not waiting for "another life".

One text is often quoted out of context to support the karmic, legalistic approach: "Work out your salvation with fear and trembling". This was written to the Philippians, whose city's wealth depended on a silver mine nearby. They had this source of treasure on their doorstep, they had only "to work it out." They were being urged to develop what God had given them, not to earn it!

REINCARNATION IN THE EARLY CHURCH

It is often asserted that reincarnation was widely accepted in the early church, but we have many letters, books etc. from people of those early days, and there is very little reference to it. It would seem that Origen, a century earlier than the Council of Nicea did believe in some form of it (*The Early Church*, by W H C Frend (SCM p.93) but was criticized for doing so, and the great Basil of Caesarea possibly believed in it too (*ibid*. p173), but as a rule it is not mentioned in any of the writings of the other great fathers of the Church. The very fact that there are one or two references to it show that it was not censored.

In fact it does not make sense to assert that there was deliberate censorship. Anybody who has read the history of that time, with all its conflicts and cross-currents will know that no one person or party could have got away with tampering with *all* the documents in a uniform way. The church in Rome in those days certainly could not have carried through such action, for it had not begun to claim the authority which it later exercised. And even if one lot of heretical books were burned, it could not have been more than a local event.

THE BIBLE DOCUMENTS

It is often asserted in New Age books that the Bible documents were tampered with after the Council of Nicea in 325 and that material acceptable to the New Age people was cut out and destroyed (especially about reincarnation). This is rubbish! For at least 150 years now the Bible has been subjected to close scrutiny, often by those who were out to de-bunk it. We now have copies of or references to the Bible from all over "the world" of that time, and a quite clear picture has emerged.

For instance we know that Polycarp, bishop in Smyrna (Turkey today) who had known St John personally, referred to the four Gospels, some letters from St Paul, 1 Peter and Hebrews. That was in about 108. In about 150 the *Diatesseron* was produced in Syria, a blending of the four Gospels into one narrative. A bit later in what we call Lyons (France), Irenaeus set out a list (canon) of the New Testament books which were regarded as authentic, very much like ours today. By 200 the New Testament was more or less fixed, although there were one or two books, such as "Revelation" which were still doubtful.

The four Gospels, then, more or less as we have them, were recognized as the essential witnesses from very early days, throughout the Roman Empire, from France to what we call Iraq, and down into Egypt. All this was long before the Council of Nicea.

We know that other Gospels circulated and had some valuable authentic material in them, but they are later and their picture of Jesus has been made to fit Gnostic ideas. For instance the accounts of the healing miracles are much more like the healings recorded in other non-Christian documents of that day.

How do we know that they are later? If we set before you three newspaper articles, one written in 1820, one in 1920 and one in today's paper, you would find it easy to say which was written when, even if there was nothing in them to give you a date. The style alone would enable you to date them. And so it is with books of those days. What with style and content, and cross references, these books can be dated pretty accurately. (See *Are the New Testament Documents Reliable?*, by F.F.Bruce)

We can be clear in our minds, then, that the four Gospels that we have are the ones which were in use within the lifetime of people who had known the first "witnesses". While there are variations in the copies which come from different places, they are minor ones, and only go to show that there has been no large-scale tampering. The Gnostic Gospels are later and while we may read them with interest, we must always test them against the Four which are in the Bible.

AGES AND AGES

The final topic at which we look in detail is the question of "AGES". Perhaps it would have been better to look at the question earlier on in the book, but it is rather an academic question and by now the reader knows what to skip!

The idea was very real to the Greeks. Hesiod tells that there was a Golden Age, when everything was ideal, the Silver Age when men grew soft, the Bronze Age when they grew violent, and then the Heroic Age which speaks for itself, and finally the Iron Age, which was the age of the Roman Empire. They thought that time was a cycle so that the Golden Age would return eventually.

On the other hand Rudolf Steiner taught that a new age had dawned about 1899. The age of darkness, the *Kali Yoga*, that had held sway for 5,000 years had come to an end, and from then on new spiritual capacities were to awaken in humanity. That is another version.

We have adapted the idea of ages in referring to "the stone age", "the space age" etc, but we mean something quite different from both the Greeks and from Steiner. However the New Age people are using it in a still deeper sense. Their concept of "a new age" is drawn from something perceived in the whole pattern of the universe. Gordon Strachan in his book *Christ and the Cosmos* spells this out in detail as noted earlier. Basically they argue that the birth of Jesus was the start of a new Age, the age of PISCES, the fish. If you look at the Greek word for fish, you will find that it is IXTHUS, and that spells *Iesou Xristos THeou `Uios Soter* - Jesus Christ son of God, Saviour - and it was the earliest sign for Christians.

Because of the way the world moves, as Gordon Strachan explains carefully, early in the next century will see the start of a new age: the Age of Aquarius, the water pourer. There are non-Christian New Agers who conclude that therefore IXTHUS is no longer relevant, and they consign the Christian Gospel to past history, looking for a new Messiah figure for the New Age. However Christian New Agers point out that the FISH comes into his own in the waters of Aquarius. Both varieties look forward with great hope to the dawn of a new Age, sure that it is going to be wonderful.

However there is nothing of this visible in the Bible as we usually know it, and therefore most Christians write all this off as unbiblical nonsense. Time in the Bible runs in a line from Creation until the Day of the Lord. Perhaps the BC-AD divide is accepted, but conventional Christians await the Day of the Lord and that is it.

There have always been extremists who have formed sects of intense people who are sure that they have worked out when the Lord will return and what will happen. Obviously St Paul had problems with this type in Thessalonica, and their modern descendants (Jehovah's Witnesses and similar groups) keep on predicting! However the main-line churches cite Matthew 24:36, "Yet about that day and hour no one knows, not even the angels in heaven, not even the Son" (i.e. not even Jesus knew). He told us to get on with the work he had given us so that we should be ready at ANY moment to face our Lord. There are many pointers, flashes of insight, and warnings in chapters like Matthew 24 and Mark 13, but when people try to work it all out in detail, they usually find that they have it wrong, and history has a sorry procession of folk who have made this mistake. Therefore the main-line churches do not say much about the Day of the Lord, even though it remains part of the basic belief: God has something lined up for the future!

KAIROS & CHRONOS

When the hopeful disciples asked the Risen Lord whether he was now going to bring in the Kingdom of God, he gave an interesting answer. To understand it, we have to note that in Greek there are two words which we translate as TIME. One is *chronos*, which means time by the clock, CHRONological time. The other word is *kairos* which means time in the sense of "the right time to do something", or "he has a beautiful sense of timing". Jesus' answer is that it is not for us to know either the *chronos* or the *kairos*, translated usually as "it is not for you to know the times and the seasons".

We might conclude therefore that the whole idea of Ages is foreign to Christian belief, there being no reference to it in the Bible.

But **WAIT A MOMENT**! The last verses in St Matthew's Gospel, so well loved, and usually read at baptisms, end with the words to which many of us have clung in times of stress: "Lo! I am with you always, even to the end of the world". That phrase "end of the world" is very interesting: "THE END" translates a Greek word made up of two parts, the first syllable is *sun* which means "together". The second syllable is a verb from *telos* which still today in Greece means "a goal". When you score a goal it is not the end of the match! The goal is something you aim at together.

This word, then, speaks to us of reaching something for which we have all been striving!

The other word in the phrase is "THE WORLD", and that translates the Greek word for AGES... well, well! He is with us up the goal of the ages.

Later when St.John wrote his Gospel, it seems that he found problems with the Hebrew idea of The KINGdom of God... many of his Greek hearers were strong republicans anyway! In Matthew, Mark and Luke, Jesus' teaching is all about the Kingdom, counteracting the exclusivist, nationalistic ideas about the Kingdom of God, and therefore about the nature of the King (Christ) who was to rule it.

In the third chapter of his Gospel, St John reports a conversation with a Jewish leader, in which Jesus speaks of the Kingdom, but by the end of the chapter the concept of "everlasting life" takes over as the main theme, and stays there for the rest of the Gospel. That is, if you read the old King James or Authorised Version. If, however, you begin to look up more modern versions you may find it is "eternal life". But you will find it hard to discover a Bible which gives the literal translation, which is THE LIFE OF THE AGES!

When Jesus says to Martha (John 11:26), "He who believes on me shall never die", the actual words are: "...believing in me certainly not dies in the age". In the various places where "for ever and ever" appears, it is "in the age of ages" or some such in the Greek. In Mark 10:30, when Jesus speaks to Peter about the future, He goes on to say that those who follow Him will have life "into the age coming, the life of ages."

So we might go on seeing where reference to AGES is hidden by translations. Where the word *is* used, the reference is rather unflatteringly to "this age".

We can, however be clear about this: that the New Testament writers were very aware of the concept of AGES! We therefore have to be careful before saying that there is no reference to Ages in the Bible!

That is not to say that we need to agree with astrologers that the universe dictates a New Age. As Jesus is King in the Kingdom (part of the meaning of "Christ" is "anointed king"), so he is Lord of the Life of the Ages. It may be that he is beginning a new stage in the world's history, and we began this book by looking at many things which point this way.

THE HOPE OF THE WORLD

After all this it is natural to ask: "What is the attraction in believing in a the dawning of a new age?" It is simply that it gives people HOPE, that basic necessity for humanity. The opposite of hope is despair, and that is a real killer. Without some "looking forward to something" we as human beings die, emotionally and physically.

In the present situation of flux and upheaval people need HOPE. The early church had that hope, as all around them the Roman Empire crumbled. That is what made them so strong in an age when cynicism and escapism were destroying civilization.

New Agers expect great upheavals at the changeover of every AGE, and see in the world today (to quote the New Testament) "the birth-pangs of the age to come". The difference between this view, and the biblical view, is in the source and location of hope. New Age teaching locates hope in getting right with creation, the life of the cosmos within each one of us, while the Bible locates hope in the Creator, revealed in Jesus Christ.

The conflict between good and evil must reach its climax... the harvest of all that has been sown. Whilst the ultimate victory was assured on Easter morning, yet there is a real battle going on, and we have our part to play. Beyond the climax of that battle lies "The Day of the Lord", and if we are wise, we do not make too many predictions about what that means.

The preaching of the Gospel to every nation is the pre-requisite to the END (Matthew 24:14, Mark 13:10), and the word there is *telos*, which means, you remember, the GOAL not the finish. This is the work which the Lord has given us to do, and which we must complete. Any belief which implies that we can sit back and wait for the stars to bring in a new age is dangerous.

Yet we must not judge movements by their extremists. If we all seek to contribute to "the pool of knowledge" those truths which we do see, and seek to discern the truth which lies behind what seems to us to be error in the contributions of the others, then maybe we can form a deeper hope in which to live and work. We will never generate much light in the world's darkness if we spend our time telling each other where s/he is wrong!

However we look at it, we are on the threshold of a new age... whether it is THE New Age or not only time will determine, and those of us who are alive now may not live to see it. It is not for us to know the "*chronos* or the *kairos*", said Jesus, but it *is* for us to keep the Light burning in a time of great upheaval, and to leave the issues with God.

PART IV LET'S EXPLORE!

15 THE JOURNEY

OUR WORLD-VIEW

The world offers a real treasury of spiritual experience. Books such as the Oxford Book of Prayer give us insights into the prayer-life of people in many religions, and these prayers ring a lot of bells with many of us, for instance:

O my God,

Only Your compassion and kindness can restore my brokenness.

My poverty nothing can enrich but Your gentleness and goodness.

Only grace from You can calm my agitation;

My frailty, Your power alone can strengthen. *(p.334)*

Such a prayer from a Moslem speaks for us all. No longer do we believe that everybody in the world should "be like me"... whether I am a Scots Presbyterian or an Irish Catholic! (However we have to admit that some Christians still DO think that everybody should be just like them or go to hell!) It is one thing to believe that in the Life of Jesus we see the fulfilment of all that is true and loving in all religions, the ultimate truth about the relationship between God and humanity. It is another to think that "my way" of expressing it is the only way.

* To believe in the ultimate truth of the Gospel does not imply that every other religious insight is wrong and diabolic.

* Wanting to share the Gospel with everybody does not mean that we have to start by telling them that every truth they have discovered so far is false.

We look out at this world, then, as a place in which there is a world of spirituality to explore. Exploring is a natural human activity, stronger in some than in others. Where would we be without explorers? Yet in our day there is little left to explore on the physical side of our planet, so that the real exploring is in the realm of human awareness.

It is no wonder then that adventurous spirits are finding out what Indians, Red Indians, Chinese and others have discovered about human life, about God and about prayer.

"Like attracts like" in this sphere of life as in all things: what people find in these various other religions depends on what they are looking for. The person for whom Jesus is a living Lord will see something very different in other religions than somebody who is money-minded. The insecure person will see them as a threat, whereas the person who is secure in faith will see where God has been preparing the way for the Gospel.

The spiritual quest is, then, the exploration of our day. Yet exploration is only the first step. The vital question in all exploration is what you DO with what you discover. We have learned that lesson, to our cost, about our earthly environment. We have learned too that exploring is dangerous, and there are always casualties. The danger is especially real if people go into strange territory unprepared, undisciplined, and unready to cope with what they discover.

One cannot emphasize enough that there is nothing intrinsically wrong in exploring God's creation, the seen or unseen parts of it. There is nothing wrong in gaining more knowledge about the universe, but it is not an adventure to be undertaken lightly. Many Christians of all varieties seem far too fearful about anything which is outwith their little framework, stuck in their own "castle" in a sort of religious paranoia.

We have also to say that too many New Agers are involved in an undisciplined gathering of dribs and drabs of healing and mystical techniques from all over the world. These may be fascinating, but there is hard work to be done before they can be used responsibly. Otherwise we find the truth of the old proverb, "a little knowledge is a dangerous thing."

MEDITATION

Take an example: Eastern and Western mysticism are based on two opposite understandings of what life is about. For the oriental, the aim of life is to separate spirit from body, in order to escape from the weary round of reincarnations. They have centuries of costly experiment behind them and have developed techniques which many western people play with. Their whole aim is to separate "pure spirit" from the taint of the body, to get past personality, emotion, desire and so on into pure undifferentiated spirit. In *How to know God, The Yoga Aphorisms of Patanjili* we read, "When the lake of the mind becomes clear and still, man knows himself as he really is, always was and always will be. He knows that he is the Atman. His 'personality', his mistaken belief in himself as a separate, unique individual disappears. 'Patanjili' is only an outer covering, like a cloak or mask, which he can assume or lay aside as he chooses. Such a man is a free, illumined soul."

The Christian understanding of meditation is very different. Meditation for us is silent communion with a PERSON... Christ. Since we worship "THE WORD MADE FLESH" there must be no question of separating the various aspects of ourselves. We are to love God with our total being. The ultimate aim is, as St Paul put it, "to know as I am known", and in that knowing my personality is raised to its height, even as I forget myself, "lost in wonder, love and praise."

At the start, we looked at the fact that it is the wonderful UNITY of spirit, intellect, psyche and body which is the mystery of life. We also noted that the nature of the devil is to "throw apart" while God in Christ is working out the unity of love around the Cross.

Therefore in Christian meditation, far from discarding all that makes up "me", the vision is "the resurrection of the body and the life everlasting", and "we shall be like HIM, for we shall see him as he is" (1 John 3:1-3). This is very different from the oriental idea of losing your identity in the ocean of Being.

Of course for Christians too there is the need to allow the old self-made personality to be destroyed, "crucified with Christ". Jesus said that those who follow him must deny self, take up the Cross and follow him, for whoever seeks to save his psyche (that is the word in the Greek New Testament) will lose it (Mark 8:34-5). To be obsessed with self-preservation is self-destructive. To forget yourself is to BE yourself. Such is Christian mystical teaching, and it obviously overlaps at points with Hindu teaching, while at the same time it has a very different goal.

On the surface both Christian and Hindu speak of one-ness as being the ultimate aim, but the oneness of love gives value to "the other", whereas the oneness of the raindrop in the ocean is quite different. So, because centuries of wisdom lie behind each tradition, it is foolish to think that one can just transpose something, such as yoga, and not cause confusion.

It is foolish on the other hand to think that we have nothing to learn from other traditions such as yoga. However that requires responsible theological thinking.

CONTRADICTIONS

It is only too easy, however, for those of us who are Christian to see ourselves through rose-tinted spectacles. We need to "see ourselves as others see us". It is no part of the Gospel that we should claim to be sinless and perfectly right!

Whatever our theories, Christian and Hindu, it is the western nations, who are seen as being Christian (whether we like it or not), which threaten to destroy the planet, using up non-renewable resources selfishly, polluting the atmosphere with emissions and so on. By contrast Africans and Orientals seem to have a deeper feeling for the earth.

Again, many Western missionaries who proclaim the "Word made flesh" appear to be strangely divorced from their bodies and from the physical side of life, while those among whom they have come to live seem more at home in the physical, earthy side of life. It is all upside down!

It is not funny, however, when one reads in "Christian books" about Hinduism and Buddhism being "of the devil", while Orientals look at the "Christian nations" and see that it is very vocal Christians in the USA who agitate for nuclear weapons and star-wars, whilst living with a level of luxury and energy greed which is destroying the world.

We come back, then, to look at our two original types of Christian, one liable to gather interesting items in the course of exploring, but in danger of confusion, while the other makes sweeping statements about other religions being demonic, as if they themselves were the only people in the world who knew the truth, all the time acting in ways that make the very name of "Christian" stink.

Our big task is to find a way through the jungle of human religious experience which neither wanders into credulity on the one hand, nor into bigotry on the other.

* We will not be carried away by what the latest New Age guru or charismatic cult figure tells us. But we will listen to all whose lives bear the stamp of truth and love.

RECOGNISING GOD AT WORK

Yes, let us explore Our Father's wonderful creation, with its interlocking systems of spiritual, psychic and physical spheres; explore it reverently, and with due regard to the hidden evils, but not obsessed with fear of them.

We claim the whole creation for God: **"The earth is the Lord's, and everything in it"** (Psalm 24:1). Whatever people have discovered about the earth, at any level, we claim for the Kingdom of God. That does not mean the sort of Christian imperialism which destroys cultures

154

which are "different". On the contrary it will mean that we discern where God is at work in them already, giving real value to all that is good in other cultures*.

We may have to reinterpret many of these discoveries, but we affirm that whatever truth has been discovered, be it by eastern guru or by communist technician, must lead to Him who is TRUTH, however *they* interpret it in terms of *their* philosophies. The fact that a truth, or a discovery, has been abused, or has even been used to harm people, does not alter that fact that set within the Kingdom of God it could be good. Think of nuclear energy for example.

As we have learned from our explorations at the geographical level, it is a serious mistake to discover a new area, and then to force our own pattern of life on it. There is a real danger of imperialism in spiritual things too! Too often Christians have done serious harm by forcing their own European culture on "natives" without regard to the real values they already have. They think they are "missionaries" converting people to Christianity, when it turns out that what they are actually doing is to make people into "little-Europeans"... and now some Americans are doing the same. Their "converts" only too often become fodder for the big industrialists, inhabitants of the terrible new city slums. Happily, there have always been some who avoided this mistake, and valued the culture in which they were proclaiming the Gospel.

Therefore we must be careful that in claiming the earth as the Lord's, we are sensitive to what the Lord has already been doing. George More told us that he had gone to India as a missionary, but found that God had been there before him, "for an awful long time!"

If we are sensitive in our explorations, we may find that He has been there before us as "The Unknown God" (Acts 17:23). The way to claim that truth for the Lord requires great sensitivity, and an understanding of the Gospel which is positive and hopeful.

* **Truth flows from one soul to another when real trust has been established, but when two people argue trying to prove one another wrong, a truth-proof barrier goes up. It is mutual trust which opens the way for exploration.**

BASE CAMP

If we are going to explore, we need a solid base camp from which to begin, so we now turn to look at what is required for this.

Without this we shall become mere esoteric dabblers. What then do we need for a base camp?

(1) We need a well thought-out intellectual framework which takes account of the experience of the past but is not in thrall to it.

(2) We need to be part of two quite different communities:

(a) *A multi-purpose community*, concerned with expressing the Gospel with regard to the whole of life, and not just with the area one feels called to explore. We need such a community to cross-check our findings, to support, encourage and sometimes to pick up the explorer, to cleanse and heal him or her. Above all we need this multi-purpose community to guard against the exploration becoming an obsession, and the explorer becoming a crank.

(b) *A community in which we can share specialist knowledge*. Here lies a common danger: FORTRESSES.

Unless we face this, we never properly begin: the danger of turning the base camp into a fortress.

One finds good, sincere people who have built a fortress around themselves and their like-minded friends. It is surrounded with a spiky hedge of biblical texts, and their constant activity is to add text to text, rule to rule, until they feel safe. From such a fortress one will never explore. Such a structure may attract frightened souls who are afraid of the uncertainties of life, whereas the healthy-minded see these uncertainties as invitations to explore.

Having such a fortress will not suit our purpose. The defences become impenetrable from the inside as well as from the outside. In fact such holy cliques become so irrelevant that nobody is even interested in attacking them. Their weakness lies in the fact that people with this fortress mentality are continually sub-dividing because of disagreement over obscure points of doctrine. Like a stag's antlers, their magnificent defences are used only against others of their kind.

In fairness one must describe yet another fortified position from which it is not likely that one will explore far. This position begins with the assumption that anything supernatural is "out of bounds". If such events are recorded in the Bible, then they are "de-mythologized", explained away. This position is very common among those whose professional life involves constant contact with other professionals whose outlook is materialistic. If they are to get promotion and acceptance, then their expression of the faith must be in terms which are as near as possible to what they think is "the scientific outlook". To admit to the supernatural would threaten their whole standing in academic, medical or social work structures. They have a "fortress" to keep the supernatural out!

Looking at these two positions, one thinks of a phrase George MacLeod of Iona used to use (was it his own?): "defending the religion of their grandmother against the science of their grandfather."

We must therefore set about establishing a base-camp from which to explore.

THE LOGOS

It is outwith the scope of such a book to provide a complete guide to the universe! Yet it would be escapism not to try to offer some contribution to forming a basis from which to explore further - provided this does not become yet another "fortress" system, from which every other system can be proved faulty!

Since many people have never explored Christian theology at all, forming their ideas of what it is about from Sunday School leftovers, it is only right that some more adult thinking should be offered. After all, who would set out to explore the world without any more geography than that which he had learned at Primary School?

Of course you may well have your own base-camp, and therefore you may look condescendingly on what I offer here. You may on the other hand have become aware that perhaps you have developed a fortress, and perhaps I can offer you a gateway out of it.

Or perhaps you have never worked anything out... in the latter case you may find this chapter useful, but only as a start. Certainly, unless one is ready to do some disciplined study and thinking, the universe may turn out to be a dangerous place to explore.

Where better to start than the opening of St John's Gospel? John was writing for people with a Greek culture, for whom the words "Messiah" (Christ) and "Son of God" were meaningless terms, or worse... misleading. We are not unfamiliar with this today!

So John begins with the term *logos* which was a well understood word for the people around him. We have come across it already in slight disguise: theoLOGY, astroLOGY, psychoLOGY etc. That is, the *logos* of God, the *logos* of the stars, the *logos* of the mind. We also know it in LOGIC. It means something like "THE MEANING BEHIND". It is not so much the noise you make with your mouth, but what you really mean, so that when people try to translate it as "the word", it refers not so much to sounds, but what it is in your inner being that you are trying to say, as in "I give you my word". The Chinese would recognize it as the *tao*.

The Gospel according to St John, then, begins with something that is almost a poem on the theme of the Logos. He is asking us to read all that follows in the light of this opening. Still today, this forms one of the best base-camps from which to explore the Gospel and the universe around it.

A FRESH START

Try to empty your mind of pre-conceptions and mis-conceptions about what Christianity is and is not. Start afresh from what St John offers us.

His Gospel begins with the words:
IN THE BEGINNING...

This is a direct quote from the first words in the Bible. John takes us right back to the basic Jewish position, which was inherited by both Christians and Moslems: **God made the world, and it is good**.

WAS THE LOGOS...

This asserts that the whole of creation is logical, consistent, with one fundamental principle running through everything. This, of course, is the basis of all true science. The psychic and spiritual spheres have their own logic. They are not irrational as some people suggest. It is not true that Christians believe in an illogical universe because of our belief in miracles, although many people suggest that we do. However God's logic is not confined to the logic familiar to humanity in its fallen state. The supernatural is not un-natural. **ALL is logical if only we can understand it.**

AND THE LOGOS WAS WITH GOD IN THE BEGINNING AND THE LOGOS WAS GOD.

Some people then, and now, think of God as being impassive, immovable, and so on. Therefore they have to bring in other beings to create the universe. John is quite clear: the Creation is the result of God's self-expression, His Word. Whatever other beings there may be and whatever processes God used (evolution or not), **it is all His Expression-work.**

158

WITHOUT HIM WAS NOT ANYTHING MADE THAT WAS MADE.

He stresses yet again that the universe, is a logical unity, there
one fundamental principle behind everything, seen and unseen:
God's Self-expression.

Everything, then, is potentially good, although, as we have seen,
evil also meets us at every level. That leads to the question as to where
Satan and the demons fit into this... and well you may ask! One may
read in the Book of Revelation of the final destruction of these entities,
and ponder as to where it all fits together. One may read in Ephesians
of how *all things are eventually to be reconciled in Christ*, and a lot
more wondering is to be done! There are some questions to which we
would not understand the answer even if we were given it. We have to
do a lot of spiritual growing before we begin to grasp any idea which
makes sense of this problem! As George MacLeod used to say: **"Follow
the light you do see and pray for more light"**.

You will receive no more light until you have followed the light
which you have already seen!

IN HIM WAS LIFE AND THAT LIFE WAS THE LIGHT OF MANKIND.

Or, as the New English Bible puts it magnificently, "all that
came to be was alive with his life". We can see that it is this LOGOS
which pushes through dead matter to create LIFE, and pushes through
animal and vegetable life to create the LIGHT, the consciousness of
humanity.

*THE LIGHT SHINES IN THE DARKNESS, AND THE DARKNESS
HAS NEVER OVERCOME IT.*

Here as elsewhere in the Bible, the negative force, darkness, just
comes into the story without explanation. How often down the centuries
it has looked as if the darkness were swallowing up all that was truly
human, all that was truly "in the image of God", but always the darkness
passes, the Neros and Hitlers of this world ("The Beast" to use the
imagery of Revelation) go from the stage, and ordinary folk go on
quietly rebuilding. In our own lives too sometimes we may have
thought that the darkness had swallowed us up. Yet it cannot, and it
never can, however deep the shadows it may cast.

THERE WAS A MAN SENT FROM GOD WHOSE NAME WAS JOHN HE CAME AS A WITNESS TO THE LIGHT, SO THAT THROUGH HIM ALL MEN MIGHT BELIEVE. HE HIMSELF WAS NOT THE LIGHT, HE CAME ONLY TO BEAR WITNESS TO THE LIGHT.

Here John the Evangelist writes about John the Baptist, who preceded Jesus, as you can read in the Gospels. He was a famous man in his day, known outwith the Bible. He proclaimed and summed up the lessons of that part of the Bible we call "The Old Testament"... the Jewish Bible.

He challenged injustice and corruption in the rulers, demanded fair dealing and justice among the people. He called on everybody firstly to face and then to turn away from the rotten-ness in the national life, making a new start in baptism. All this was because he saw that the Messiah (the king), long promised in the Bible, was about to arrive. We are faced here with the truth that the moral law is at the heart of the human story. When the moral law is broken, destructive forces are released, and we suffer. God is concerned to set this right, not by waving a magic wand to stop war and injustice, but by seeking to win people to live His Way.

THE TRUE LIGHT WHICH GIVES LIGHT TO EVERY MAN WAS COMING INTO THE WORLD. That can also be translated: *THIS WAS THE TRUE LIGHT THAT GIVES LIGHT TO EVERY MAN WHO COMES INTO THE WORLD.*

Whichever version you choose, there is the emphasis that everybody, prehistoric cave-man, atheistic space-man, Australian aborigine, Eskimo, the lot, know something of that light. Mentally handicapped children know it too! It is there in every religion, every philosophy, even if it is atheistic. You can't get away from it! It will shine through somewhere!

Now, says John, the embodiment of that light was coming into the world, not another witness like the Baptist... or like the other great souls who have sought to point to the light, but the Light in Person.

HE WAS IN THE WORLD, AND THOUGH THE WORLD WAS MADE THROUGH HIM, THE WORLD DID NOT KNOW HIM.

There is the tragedy: we do not recognize that which is our true nature. We try to find our identity in our own way. As individuals and as nations, in all sorts of ways, we miss the point of being human.

Confronted with true man and true God we do not recognize Him. Somebody once said: "Jesus is what man means by 'GOD' and what God means by 'MAN'."

About the last thing people mean when they say "GOD" is: **'suffering-love'.** The usual pictures of God tend to be in terms of great kings, monstrous beasts, the sun... or as ultimate idea, universal spirit and so on. The result was that humanity could not recognize the Light when they saw it, that is the human tragedy.

HE CAME TO HIS OWN BUT HIS OWN DID NOT RECOGNIZE HIM.

Even though for centuries, as recorded in the Old Testament, God had struggled to make Himself known, by preparing for Himself a people who knew Him, when it came to the point they did not. This points us to something very important in the God-humanity relationship: We may call God "Almighty", (even though the original name *El Shaddai* meant All-Sufficient), but that does not mean that He will force people to obey Him, force us to to stop war, to be just and so on. We are free to say NO.

YET TO ALL WHO RECEIVED HIM, TO THOSE WHO BELIEVED IN HIS NAME, HE GAVE THE RIGHT TO BECOME THE CHILDREN OF GOD, CHILDREN BORN NOT OF NATURAL DESCENT, NOR OF HUMAN DECISION, OR A HUSBAND'S WILL, BUT BORN OF GOD.

Those who recognize the authority of Jesus ("believe in his Name") get a fresh start, and come to know their true nature as God's children. This teaching, in bad odour because of excesses by some "born-again Christians", is vital! When the Light has pierced the darkness of sin and confusion and meets the light hidden deep down in the human heart, so that the lost soul recognizes the Light, there is a "new birth", and seeds of a new life are sown... a real "virgin birth" in ordinary folk.

It is not an emotional experience, "engineered" by some powerful orator, but a new element introduced into the life that is ready to receive it. The "new birth" is not to be confused with a "conversion experience" which may or may not follow it.

Nor is it dependent on believing the whole of Christian doctrine. It is only AFTER new birth has happened that the various doctrines begin to make sense. It is often suggested that you have to believe

FIRST, and then the new life will begin, but it is only those who hav
been "fertilized" by God's Spirit who can see what it is all about.

THE WORD WAS MADE FLESH AND LIVED A WHILE AMONG U
The *Logos*, God's Self-expression came through the medium
humanity. Not in a Super-man, who would not be truly human, nor ye
in an appearance of humanity, but in real human flesh, as John says
more detail in the opening of his first Letter. Summed up in that huma
life is the whole glory and tragedy of life, and in that life we discove
the secret of God which in the Jewish temple was hidden behind th
curtain of the Holy Place.

COMMON ERRORS

There are several ways in which we can get confused:
There are many stories the world over of gods coming to earth, and
mortals begotten of human women by some god, and therefore calle
sons of a god. That is not what we mean by Jesus being "Son of God"
Jesus is a historical person whose coming is dated whereas the othe
myths of gods in human guise are "once upon a time" stories. It is as
human consciousness was groping for this truth in many places, but
Jesus the truth finally dawned. Nowhere else is such a being dated
human history, recorded by people of his time. Jesus is a historica
person, not a fairy story.

Many great souls have pointed god-wards, or like the Buddha
have made their protest against idol-worship (later to be made into idol
themselves, no doubt to their horror!). Yet they never claimed to be go
Jesus did, and his disciples claimed so too for him. It is not that Jesu
taught people about God - he lived, and died, the Life of God.

Another error is to start by assuming you know what the wor
g-o-d means and you then try to see in what way Jesus was divine
Endless argument has taken place trying to do this. Begin at the othe
end: look at what you can understand: the Man Jesus. Then, bit by b
you will begin to see what divinity means... what God is like.

SUPERMAN?
Even many well-meaning Christians have undone th
"incarnation" (which means, becoming flesh) by taking the divinity o
Jesus to mean that he must be somehow different from us, a super-man
a super-miracle-worker and so on. In doing this, they have tried to tur

162

him back into the sort of figure he refused to be, instead of accepting him as one who comes to us "from underneath", from the depths of human sin and suffering, from among the poor, among those who suffer injustice. (In this book, "he" is written with a small letter when it refers to Jesus, not because he was not God, but to stress God's determination really to "put on our human nature" in the person of Jesus.)

Even those of us who are convinced Christians have to look again and again at the "offence" of such a God, allowing ourselves to be challenged by a God who identifies with the poor, the outcast, the sinners... us. **That is the LOGOS!**

GO FURTHER ON!

From that basis perhaps *you* can go on to explore, as St John does in his Gospel, the life, death and resurrection of Jesus, and discover what it means for you.

It is not a matter of accepting the dogmas of the past, but rather of discovering gladly those truths which the men and women of old tried to put into words, knowing that no words can fully describe God. As Lao Tse said:

"The Tao which can be described is not the Tao".

In other words: "No graven images"... or intellectual idols either! God is too great for "words".

HAPPY EXPLORING!

FOR FURTHER EXPLORATION

Most of those reading this book will be European by origin; we will function best if we keep in contact with our roots, when we try to understand the life of Jesus (although he was not European!) Our exploring will then have a firm base from which to begin.

On the Christian Life, try *GROWING KNOWING JESUS*, by Ian Cowie (St Andrew Press).

On the Hindu area, try *THE MARRIAGE OF EAST AND WEST*, by Bede Griffiths, a Benedictine monk (Fount Books). He now has a number of books exploring further.

On Japanese Zen, try *SILENT MUSIC*, by William Johnston, a Jesuit (Fount Books).

On what we usually refer to as "animism" in Africa, try *CHRISTIANITY REDISCOVERED* by Vincent O'Donovan (SCM Press).